Dating

MAKES YOU
WANT TO Die

(But You Have to Do It Anyway)

Daniel
Holloway

&

Dorothy
Robinson

COLLINS LIVING
An Imprint of HarperCollins Publishers

HarperCollins books may be purchased for educational, business, or
sales promotional use. For information, please write: Special Markets Department,
HarperCollins Publishers, 10 East 53rd Street, New York, NY 10022.

FIRST EDITION

Designed by Jennifer Ann Daddio

Library of Congress Cataloging-in-Publication Data

Holloway, Daniel.
Dating makes you want to die : but you have to do it anyway /
by Daniel Holloway and Dorothy Robinson.—1st ed.
p. cm.
ISBN 978-0-06-145650-3
1. Dating (Social customs)—Humor. 2. Man-woman relationships—Humor.
I. Robinson, Dorothy (Dorothy N.) II. Title.
HQ801.H723 2008
306.73—dc22
2008011615

08 09 10 11 12   OV/RRD   10 9 8 7 6 5 4 3 2 1

CONTENTS

In the ancient times—before Al Gore invented the Internet—finding a forever mate was simple. Two postpubescent youngsters would get together if their parents and community thought it was appropriate. A boy would come over to "call," and he and his young lady of choice would sit on the front porch, holding hands. He would wear overalls and have dreams of seeing the big city. She would wear a bow in her hair and be fertile but chaste. If she had all her teeth and good birthing hips, the boy would ask the girl's father for her hand. As long as she didn't die of consumption and he didn't run off to join the merchant marine, the two would live happily ever after and die at forty.

But happily ever after isn't so easy anymore. Courting is now called "dating," and this unfortunate yet necessary social endeavor now induces panic attacks and therapist visits. The ritual of courtship has been replaced by the ritual of obsessively updating your online profile. That dainty young miss on the front porch? She's now a bitchy dragon woman in middle management who would rather build a spreadsheet than track down a boyfriend. The earnest little guy? He's evolved into a hair-plugged meatface who desperately tries to bang spring breakers in Panama City Beach.

That Which Needs Doing

eHarmony commercials and poorly written sitcoms might make it seem like dating is a perfectly fine thing to get involved in. Don't be fooled. The fact is most people don't want to date. If given the choice between a night watching *CSI: Miami* or going to "meet for coffee" with a complete stranger, most people would much prefer to gaze upon the pockmarked visage of David Caruso for an hour. You, like us, have probably gone on dates that make you hate humanity (and your parents) for bringing you into this soulless world where someone would actually contemplate going out with a human being who has the social graces of a wolf-child.

But as our subtitle says, you have to do it anyway, which begs the question: when you can't avoid a horrific experience (like, say, middle-school gym class), how do you survive it?

Well, you don't. You die. We die. Even George Clooney will die someday (though not until he's reached the age of 491, brought peace to the Eastern world, and discovered the lost city of Atlantis). But the point is, you don't have to die alone.

What's that? You're only in your twenties? You're too busy trying to score a big bag of powdered drugs and decipher the key plot points of *Lost* to worry about dying? Well, you're a liar. We know you. You came of age in a time of terrorism, a time of nuclear proliferation, a time of Bill O'Reilly. You're more worried about dying alone than your grandma in the home is—and she *is* alone.

You need to date. Truth be told—and we will always tell you the truth, like it or not—dating is hard but not complicated. Every step of a relationship is like that part in *Indiana Jones and the Last Crusade* where Indy can step only on the letters that spell the Latin name of God, or else be consumed by the bottomless cavern. Bottomless caverns are no fun, as anyone who's ever made love to Perez Hilton can attest to. But lest you, like Indy, forget your dead-language training and make a near-fatal misstep, pay attention. This book will guide you step-by-step through the chasm of romance to the holy grail of partnerhood. You will learn how to meet an attractive and reasonably intelligent member of the opposite sex, how to woo that person, how to keep it up even after you've lost your will to woo, and how to hold on to the object of your affection as he faces the wandering-eye temptation of short skirts and she's dazzled by six-pack abs and you face the temptation of letting your gym membership lapse.

But why this book? Why not just borrow your divorcée mom's dog-eared copy *of Men Are from Mars, Women Are from Venus* or your younger sister's copy of *He's Just Not That Into You*?

Because those books suck. They will create a pit of despair in your stomach that will hurt worse than any rejection you've ever suffered at the hands of the opposite sex. Most dating books are a mixed drink made with equal parts hubris and phoniness. Anyone who thinks their graduate degree or tour of duty as a cable TV writer earns them the right to be treated like St. John the

Revelator with regard to their dating life is feeding you a line of crap—and anyone who pretends to care about whether you succeed or fail at the game of love is feeding you an even bigger line of crap. Us? We prefer our mixed drinks made with gin and more gin. We will be straight with you. Our job isn't to tell you what you want to hear and then talk a lot of smack about you behind your back. That's the job of the last person you went out with.

Given that, are you really so keen on waiting to catch a pearl of wisdom as it drops from Dr. Phil's mustachioed lips? If so, dig out your receipt and take this book back to Barnes & Noble. Plenty of other titles that are perfect for you are clogging the shelves there. You won't feel entirely comfortable reading them in front of other people, but, hey, clearly you don't want to learn how to meet your own special version of a life partner. You'd rather listen to *Love Smart* on your iPod and reenact the speed-dating scene from *The 40-Year-Old Virgin*.

Incredible Drinking Buddies

See, *Dating Makes You Want to Die* is like an affable hipster alcoholic with good common sense and a killer music collection who is still establishment enough to occasionally shop at Gap. Simply put, this is an antidating book but still a dating book. It's an antirelationship book that will show you what being in a relationship is all about. How clever, no?

We dish our love tough and our advice as take it or leave it. And you will leave some of it. The infuriating thing about people is that they're all different. Some prefer *MADtv* to *Saturday Night Live*. Some prefer Cracked to *Mad* magazine. And some would rather read *The Mad Bathroom Companion* than *Mad About the '90s*.

The many-colored jewels of humanity all shine brightly in God's crown (or something like that), but there's no pleasing everyone.

Just let us help you. We want you to read this, feel normal, and understand that it's okay to hate dating. You remember normal, don't you? It's that thing you never, ever felt your entire childhood (until the day when you discovered weed and felt sort of normal—but also sort of funny—for the first time ever). Like an old-media methadone, we will help get you back to that sort-of normal place without having to swing by the drug clinic on the way to your Pilates class. It's that easy. All you have to do is read on, brave dater, read on.

ONE

A FORTRESS UNTO ITSELF:

The Single

You do not let someone else dictate your happiness. You come home whenever you damn well please. You have hobbies. You spend late nights at work without worry and haven't taken a vacation since 2003. You tell anyone who will listen that you're deliriously happy. You can't remember the last time you changed your sheets. The only person's birthday you have to remember is your mother's. You repeatedly make out with people whose last names you don't know and whose first names are equally iffy. When your confused and desperate friends ask you for dating advice, you make references to your last ex (you know, the one from three years ago). You go to the gym. You are the first to show up for parties. Heck, you even have time to think of witty RSVPs to the Evite. You are the go-to person when someone needs help moving into a new apartment or needs someone to post bail. You, dear reader, are the Single.

And you are miserable.

Better than the Chair

First thing first: It's important to remember that being single is not the death sentence that your mother makes it out to be. Sure, at your age, most of the good men and women are already snatched up by people more together than you, and you're not getting better—you're just getting older. But hope is not lost, miserable single person. Let's look at a few characteristics that define who you are and what's horribly, horribly wrong with you—and show you how to fix them.

· ·

HE SAYS/SHE SAYS

Should you hate yourself for being single?

She Says: No! Somehow we've all been programmed to believe that if you haven't already gotten married on a Disney cruise, popped out two children by thirty, live in a subdivision, and plan all-inclusive vacations to Mexico, where the only exotic people you meet are from Idaho (you've never met anyone from Idaho before!), there is something wrong with you. Well, okay, so your mother probably thinks there is something wrong with you—but that doesn't mean you should. Why in the world are you supposed to hate yourself because someone with nothing better to do hasn't asked you to get married and live a boring life watching cable on your La-Z-Boy? No. You should *love* yourself because of this.

Single women have everything going for them—there is a world of possibility ahead of them. Every single man you encounter knows he can try to get into your pants without getting smacked down by a boyfriend/husband. But talking to these eager men about how you hate yourself because you're single means that you will always, always be single. They won't jump up and say, "You hate being single, too? Let's make babies together, hot stuff!" No, they will back away and talk to the confident single girl who seems like she might be fun to hang out with.

Sure, you want to share your life with someone. That's a nice thought. But hating yourself because that hasn't happened yet only leads to overeating, depression, and wearing sweatpants everywhere you go. And you can let that happen only once you're married. Being a downer means that other downers will want to be around you, and doubling that Prozac prescription is pricey.

He Says: Yes!

To be single is to hate yourself. Clearly, everyone else in the world hates you. If they didn't, you'd be dating someone already.

But as any self-help book written since the mid-'60s will you tell you, you need to avoid that kind of negative thinking, right? Wrong. Self-loathing is a great motivator for self-improvement.

Tired of hearing you bitch and moan about your weight issues and abject loneliness, your friends will try to tell you that you're just fine. Don't listen to them. They're only saying that because they're deluding themselves. After all, if you suck, that means they, as the only people willing to spend time with you, suck by proxy. You are the only one who knows your own heart—and deep down, you know that it beats inside the body of a pathetic, unlovable loser.

But simply acknowledging your own shittiness is not enough. Life, dear reader, is like those ads in Archie comic books where a bully kicks sand in a dweeb's face, so the dweeb buys a home gym, buffs up, then kicks the bully's ass. You, self-hating single, have kicked sand in your own face—and it motivated you to go out and buy a home gym of the mind (this book). Now that you have the tools necessary to fix yourself, cling to that self-loathing until you're fixed. Use it to fuel the fires needed to get yourself in datable shape—new haircut, hot jeans, and some Proactiv Solution for that unsightly business happening on your left cheek. Soon, when you look in the mirror and see a fresh, fuckable you, you'll be glad you made yourself feel like ass.

· ·

Rome wasn't built in a day, and getting laid isn't as easy as getting kicked out of a bar. It's going to take some time, some determination, and some nights out. Look, we all know it's so much nicer to order Chinese, hang out on the couch, and send witty text messages about *Grey's Anatomy* or the *Sunday Night Football* game to your friends. But from this point on, it's important that you read semicarefully and listen to us if you ever want to be in a semihealthy relationship with another human being. Please note that not all of these pointers will pertain to you. If they do, we are sad to say that we cannot help you and it's probably for the best that you just go back to being a creepy shut-in. But for the rest of you, listen and learn. After all, if you can trust a Russian cabdriver with your life, you may as well trust us, too.

. . . .

Quiz

Are you ready to date? Take this quiz to find out.

When you think about actually trying to meet someone. You . . .

1. Sigh. You don't want to meet anyone else! Why would you? Your ex was a flawless pièce de résistance of sexitude and wantonness, but with the domestic skills of Betty Crocker or the athleticism of Roger Federer. Trying to find someone even close is an exercise in futility.
2. Keep thinking about the prospect. Then open your fridge, look around, and close it. Think about meeting the prospect some more. Can't decide if you would rather meet someone or make that box of Kraft Macaroni and Cheese for dinner.
3. Get all warm and fuzzy inside. Yes! Dating! Love love love to date! Yes! Give it to you! You would kill just for the prospect of sharing an appetizer at Macaroni Grill with someone, anyone.

Your friends try to set you up with a friend of theirs from the office. You . . .

1. Smack them straight across the face. How dare they try to infringe on this period of mourning that you've been in the past year for, as you describe the ex, "your cherished one." How dare they!
2. Laugh. Say no. Then think about it. Then open your fridge, look around, and close it. Think some more. Call back and agree as long as you can meet in a small group setting and your friend's friend isn't what is described as "having a great personality."
3. Jump at the chance. Ask for the friend's work e-mail and write them with the fever of a consumption victim on their deathbed. Google-stalk them. Then Yahoo!-stalk them because sometimes, just sometimes, Yahoo! searches dig up more. Through your thorough research, find out where they went to school and what their extracurricular activities were, and take notes so you can ask about them later.

A former fling calls you up to announce they're in town and ask you out for a drink. You . . .

1. Say, "Four years too late, bub. No more nooky from this cookie. This body is now a shrine to the holiness of 'my cherished one.' To have you dirty it with your immoral paws would be sacrilege of the highest order."
2. Say sure. Grab a drink, wind up at your house, do the familiar deed, grab coffee in the morning, then never

talk to them until the next time they "come through town."

3. Scream into the phone with the excitement of a preteen who just found out he'll be on *American Idol*. Accept. Blow your credit limit on new clothes and shoes for the event. Start a juice fast so you'll be at your slimmest when you see each other again. Thanks to the lack of solid food in your system, you get too hammered after two drinks, and then blubber on about how they stopped calling you and how only through months of therapy did you regain your self-esteem.

You've been single for . . .

1. Ha. Please, you're not single. You call this a "holding period" until your "cherished one" comes to his or her senses and comes back to you.
2. A few months (okay, maybe more. But you're cool with it—kinda).
3. Too long! You've never known such abject loneliness and terror.

When your mom inquires about your dating life you . . .

1. Ask her if she remembers that time your "cherished one" gave her that Longaberger basket for Christmas, and then ask her to send it to you so you can add it to your collection of mementos past.
2. Roll your eyes. Then tell her straight up that there aren't

any prospects at the moment, but that, don't worry, you aren't gay and, no, you don't want to be set up with that guy/gal from synagogue/church/farmers' market, thankyouverymuch.

3. Spend four hours chatting with her about how you saw someone at a bus stop that you thought *could* have potential. Inquire about the neighbor's kid you went to high school with and if they're divorced yet.

When you have a conversation with an attractive bartender you . . .

1. Talk about your "cherished one" and why you think they left you. Really, why? WHY? WWHHHYYYY????
2. Flirt relentlessly with the bartender, who gives you just enough attention to keep you hooked and run up your bar tab. When you're given the boot at closing time, you leave a two-dollar tip and never go to that bar again.
3. Sit down at the bar directly across from the bartender and chat away—every single night for the next seven months.

When you think about your last relationship you . . .

1. Cry.
2. Shrug.
3. Wonder why your ex hasn't come crawling back to you yet.

Mostly 1s

You aren't ready to date again—at all. You are too attached to your ex to even contemplate going out with another human being. And if you somehow manage to go on a date, the person will end up hating you for constantly mentioning your ex. Wait it out until the pain of your breakup subsides, or write a rambling novel about your lost love. At the book signing, your ex might show up and/or put a restraining order against you. At the very least, you have a book to remember all the good times, right?

Mostly 2s

The good news: you seem well adjusted and cool enough to contemplate spending a few hours with another human being. Congrats! You might hate going out with someone who you know deep down won't go anywhere, but you'll be able to regain some of your game. After all, practice—even practice with complete morons—makes perfect.

Mostly 3s

You are an unstoppable, voracious dating tiger! Hear you roar! However, despite your amazing (and creepy) enthusiasm, this is not a good thing. You are so unbalanced when it comes to this whole dating thing that you scare and put off everyone around you (including us). Remember: Everyone wants to date someone cool. No one wants to date someone who treats a dinner at Macaroni Grill like dining with the queen. Chill out. Don't approach dating like you're taking your GREs. Read more to learn how to balance your emotions so that you can approach the dating life like the cynic you have somehow avoided becoming.

· ·

Why You Aren't Having Sex

REASON #1: SLAVISH DEVOTION TO YOUR JOB GETS YOU NOTHING BUT A PAYCHECK

We love that you know how to make a killer PowerPoint presentation and have convinced yourself that corporate retreats are just like your childhood summers at Camp Blue Star. It's adorable. The joy you get from leaving holiday gifts for the office cleaning person shows that you're kind. But the fact that you're usually at work late enough to give them in person belies a dark truth: you aren't single; you're dating your job.

Working is a privilege. Your grandfather worked sixteen-hour days in the salt mine/cannery/slaughterhouse. Your father spent months at a time on the road selling electric fans and ham radios. You were raised with a Protestant work ethic, even though you're Jewish. To you, hard work is its own reward.

But it's not getting you laid.

Don't believe us? Then believe that tiny voice in your head. Hear it? It's saying, "The IT guy knows I've been looking at Internet porn. My severance papers are sitting in a file somewhere."

Your remedy

You, career guy or gal, need to focus a little more on members of the opposite sex who don't vacuum under your desk and aren't made of 300 dpi. If you don't want to do it for yourself, do it for your job—because that IT guy really is out to get you. So stop checking your office e-mail before your Match.com account. Stop being the first one in and the last one out and always volunteering for big projects. If you do manage to meet someone in the two hours of free time you have a week, it won't matter. They don't want to be with someone who's physically attracted to their BlackBerry.

Stop fooling yourself by thinking that your manager will notice that you're working harder than your colleagues and respond by lightening your load. In reality, he'll just give you more work. This is known as Dilbert's Paradox—and there's only one way to escape it.

Stop being so goddamn reliable. You need to roll in late, leave early, and blow a few assignments. Your boss will think twice about saddling you with a big last-second project if your next presentation is a three-minute slide show featuring pictures of your coworkers set to the tune of John Fogerty's "Centerfield." We know this goes against your nature, but just start thinking of work the way you think of your mother—and ignore it.

REASON #2: FAILURE TO ROCK

Your roommates are awesome. They never borrow your stuff, always keep the fridge well stocked, and don't ask you to contribute a dime toward rent. They're also your parents.

We respect your reluctance to grow up. The world of adults is a frightening place full of wise investments and three-drink limits. But the fact that your mom still packs you the same lunch that she did fifteen years ago is creepy. And bologna sandwiches on Roman Meal bread aren't even that good.

In the film *Failure to Launch*, Matthew McConaughey plays a thirtysomething man who still lives with his implausible parents, Kathy Bates and Terry Bradshaw. *Failure* has an important lesson to offer: unless you're *People* magazine's Sexiest Man Alive, nobody's going to hook up with you in the same bed you peed in when you were eight years old. And although we don't like to harp on it—as we all know our parents are on this earth to cater to our needs—think about your folks for a second. Do they really want to hear you masturbate into a sock through the thin walls of the home they spent a lifetime working to build? No. They want to watch their QVC in peace.

Your remedy

You need a room of your own. It seems so simple, doesn't it? But so many people in their twenties are stuck in the kitsch-filled, free-cable vortex that is known as "my mom's." Stop making excuses. Yes, it sucks that half of your paycheck will go to a sketchy landlord who you're sure has somehow rigged a video camera in your bedroom. But you can afford it. If a refugee from the Togolese Republic can sneak into the country with his five kids and score a two-bedroom apartment, you can, too. It's true: you will never wash your face with a clean washcloth ever again, and you will be paying off credit card debt until you die. But you can bring someone home to bone without your parents walking in. This means it must be done.

There's this Web site you should check out. It's called Craigslist.org. We're pretty sure you've heard of it. It's where crazy people who live in shitty apartments and are desperate for a roommate go to find people like you. Set your price, click on the first listing you see, and take it. It doesn't have to be as nice as the "artist's loft" your friend in marketing just bought in the rapidly gentrifying neighborhood downtown. It just needs to not have fire engine or pony wallpaper in the bedroom. You won't be awakened in time for morning omelets, but your new roommate will have a psychotic stepbrother and a creepy neurological disorder that will make you feel better about yourself.

REASON #3: YOU LOOK LIKE SOMEONE WHO COULD USE A COCKTAIL

When you were in high school there were only two types of kids who didn't think it was the most awesome thing in the world that the Puerto Rican guy at Mike's Beer Barn would sell you a twelve-pack of Schaefer because your best friend had a nice rack: Christians and straight-edgers. And both were scary.

You, dear reader, were not one of these people. They grew up to be youth pastors and homeless folks. You grew up to be a bright, charming contributor to society with enough disposable income to buy this book. But you know where you screwed up? You stopped letting go once in a while.

Somewhere along the way, you lost the will to get tanked. Your chemical dependencies used to make you the life of the party. You always had a beer in the fridge. Friends could come over and smoke from the comfort of your sofa. You knew a guy who knew a guy. And people loved you for it. It was the kind of love that only someone who's always ready to party knows. And you gave it up for what? Health? Longevity? Marathon training? Personal fulfillment? A Jedi craves not these things.

Your remedy

You need a cocktail. Alcohol is the lubricant that turns the path to the bedroom into a Slip 'N Slide. Members of the opposite sex don't want to have a latte with you. They want to see what you're like when you don't know when to say when. Most relationships begin as dates gone too far, and most dates gone too far begin with one drink too many. Bars are the single's Shangri-la. We aren't sure of the statistics, but probably around, oh, every single person on the face of this earth has gotten some play by simply strolling into a drinking establishment and getting shit-faced. You cannot beat these unsupported odds.

When you don't drink, you're committing yourself to a lifetime of solitude (and health, of course. But that is neither here nor there). So when you finally do become old and infirm, who will be there to take care of you? Not your spouse, and definitely not your bartender. You have friends who are the same gender as you. Make one of them (just one—large groups can intimidate attractive, sex-hungry strangers; more on that later) your bar buddy. That way, as your freewheeling twenties and thirties finally catch up with you, you'll have someone to share your decline with.

REASON #4: YOU'RE CUT OFF

Maybe you just took reason #3 a little too far and now you're wasted. You wake up in the morning, smoke a joint, roll into work a half hour late and leave a half hour early for happy hour (second happy hour, actually, if you count the two gin and tonics you had at lunch). Your tongue is a permanent shade of yellow, and you haven't had a bowel movement in almost a week. Your drug dealer goes to school with your niece and asked if you could introduce them. You said yes. Now your niece lives in a different state.

What you do isn't partying or having a "night on the town." Parties are fun. Nights out are good for the single's soul. People make out in corners and take cabs home together at parties. Nights out increase the potential of meeting someone tenfold. Now when you're drinking, nobody gets anywhere near you. They stand ten feet away and wonder if you just pooped your pants.

Your remedy

For God's sake, clean yourself up. Try this exercise: Every time you feel the urge to fix yourself a drink, rip off one of your fingernails instead. When you run out of fingernails (you will), start on the toes. Now cover the tips of your digits in Band-Aids. Once they heal, you're allowed to drink again. That should give you enough time to rethink your life. If that seems a tad too intense for your "few glasses of wine after work" problem, drink a glass of water in between every alcoholic beverage for a few months. This way you're hydrating and keeping yourself sober enough so you don't feel the need to start crying about your ex (which makes people hate you, by the way).

REASON #5: YOU DON'T KNOW HOW TO DRESS

There is one cardinal rule of fashion. No, it's not "God made dirt, so dirt don't hurt." It's "everyone looks fuckable in a good pair of jeans and a formfitting T-shirt." Lately, you've been breaking that rule (sorry, but nobody looks fuckable in a baggy pair of sweatpants with "Ohio State Buckeyes" printed across the rear end). You, dear single, forgot how to clean yourself up.

The thing is, you look good when you're in a relationship because your boy- or girlfriend dresses you up like a department store mannequin. But it's a vicious, never-ending cycle. You don't have someone to tell you what to wear, so you don't know what to wear—so you'll never get someone to tell you what to wear (confusing, we know).

Your remedy

To get in the game, you need to accrue a little "me debt." Sure, you still haven't paid off your college loans, but you're an adult now—everyone has debt. Not having debt makes you different. And who wants that? You want to look like everyone else because everyone else is getting action.

Enlist the help of a good girl or guy friend (not your drinking pal), up the limit on your credit card, and head to H & M or a store that has boot-cut Levi's and some expensive T-shirts. What? You think it's insane to spend more than twenty dollars on a T-shirt? Do you think that guy or girl you see in the coffee shop on your days off and has that funky style you admire is a bargain shopper? No. They have a thing called a "trust fund" (why else are they hanging out at coffee shops when everyone else in the world is working? Think about it). Their bohemian chic look costs more than your life.

Believe us, it takes more money than you ever thought was possible to spend on items that were made for seven cents by child laborers. But you need to look sharp. And it's important to look sharp every time you go outside. Although you might have the kind soul of Mother Teresa with the wit of Mel Brooks, no one is going to see that if they think you are going to ask them to spare some change.

So go shopping. When you're doing that lame dance-around-shimmy in the dressing room because you think you look like the hottest thing on earth, that is the outfit you should buy. Don't even look at the price tag. Because remember: once you've bagged a member of the opposite sex, consolidating your debt can be a fun project to tackle as a couple.

. . . .

Cut Your Hair

You are a subtly nuanced individual with a complex personality, special talents, and a better sense of humor than most working comedians. Luckily for you, all of your unique character traits are expressed through your hairstyle. Sporting the right 'do shows the world who you are and what the opposite sex thinks of you.

SHAVED HEAD

She Thinks: He's going bald, but not willing to throw down $2K for plugs. He'll be attentive and always grateful for my presence because his best days are behind him.

He Thinks: If she's not a lesbian, she's a white supremacist.

LONG HAIR

She Thinks: He's out of touch with reality. He's probably had his hair at this length since junior high, and he's not changing it for any woman. He's also not changing it for any job, so I'll probably have to pick up brunch.

He Thinks: Soft like the rabbits! Wait. Soft like the high-maintenance, three-hours-to-get-ready rabbit.

POMPADOUR

She Thinks: He will spend more time styling his hair than listening to me. I don't want to even think about what that kind of product will do to my pillowcases.

He Thinks: Gay? Or still stuck in her K.D. Lang fetish? Interesting.

PIGTAILS

She Thinks: He's gay and still stuck in the tenth grade.

He Thinks: She's probably so desperate that she'll play to my secret desire to bang an underage Britney Spears in her "Oops! . . . I Did It Again" video. Creepy score!

She thinks: Douche.

He thinks: I will never, ever tell my friends about having sex with you.

REASON #6: YOUR LOVE OF MITTENS

Sure, your cat loves you like no creature has ever loved you. But if you find yourself talking to your cat more than to other human beings, it's a problem. Also, your hair smells like cat litter. Nobody—not even kitty—finds that attractive.

Your remedy

We suggest putting Mittens down. No, not that "down" (even we aren't that sick). Put her down on the sofa, get dressed up, and go out. We promise, no matter how much you think she will, your cat is not going to miss you that much. She'll make it the four hours you are gone. Promise. Still feel guilty? Throw her some catnip. It will take her mind off ripping your couch to shreds—for a few minutes, anyway.

REASON #7: YOU HAVE A VAST SOCIAL NETWORK—IN YOUR INTERNET GAMING LIFE

You, Captain Solaris, and Robstank99 are the most formidable supergroup in Champion City. Your characters are each at level

50, and there is no mission you're not willing to devote hours to completing. You guys totally rock the online role-playing game *City of Heroes*.

You do not, however, rock the offline role-playing game of life. If your longest conversations in the physical realm are with the earnest Pakistani at the 7-Eleven you see every night to refuel on Mountain Dew, you need to relearn the art of conversation. Why? Because Captain Solaris isn't going to get your rocks off. If he does, maybe you should make a therapist's office your first port of call when you begin navigating the world outside your apartment.

Your remedy

Communicating doesn't mean researching the definitions for LOL, LMAO, and ROTFLMAO. We know adjusting to the outside world is difficult. People may not react to your face as enthusiastically as they do to your Internet avatar. So do something where the other person is required to be nice to you. Join a cooking class. Sign up for a college course. Go to the local Isuzu or Volkswagen dealership and pretend to shop for a moderately priced hatchback. It might not stop you from being single, but it will help you learn how to speak out loud again. So if you actually meet someone you find attractive, you won't just stand there, saying nothing and miming like you are at a keyboard.

REASON #8: YOUR FRIENDS—YOU LOVE THEM, BUT NO ONE ELSE DOES

Your buddies are hilarious. Remember that time when you passed out and Afshin put his naked balls in your mouth? Or when Karen got wasted and made out with the hot dog vendor for a free foot-long and can of Fresca?

These were all good, good times. Your friends "get you" more than anyone else does, and you guys are going to be BFF 4-eva. But the more you depend on them for fun and excitement, the less you try to find someone who will actually touch your naked body (that one wild weekend in Cancún where you and your best pal "experimented" doesn't count). Yes, you are single, and yes, you need friends to spend time with—but if you aren't accepting dates because you promised Ricky to help him get to the seventh level in *Street Fighter*, you will be cemented, forever, as the helpful single friend. Ricky, no matter how much you think he is devoted to *Street Fighter*, would rather get some tail.

Your remedy

Your friends will understand that you need to skip Saturday brunch or the weekly *Heroes* viewing party to get some play. They are your friends. Just tell them that you need to suck some face with a living, breathing person. Deep down, they know that although watching *Heroes* while eating Fritos is fun, dry humping is funner. To ease the sting (there is always a sting factor with this slight), make vague promises of bringing your new buddy over, and then dodge your friends when they try to make set plans for a meet-up.

Finishing Off

Paul Simon once said, "I am a rock, I am an island." To him, we say, "It's time you open your ports to visitors." Believe you us, it's okay to be single. Everyone, at one point in their lives, has been single—even Tommy Lee. And even the most fucked-up people in the world find someone equally fucked up. Just look at Tori Spelling and Dean McDermott, Tom Arnold and Roseanne, Arnold Schwarzenegger and Maria Shriver. Heck, even the Siamese twins Chang and Eng got married. You might hate yourself because you're single and have a muffin-top, but at least you don't have to share your internal organs with your twin, right?

Singles eventually get savvy enough to turn their fate of eternal solitude around. But you aren't savvy, and that is why we love you. And you know what? Despite all odds, someone else will love you, too. They really will. Just give it some time, and try out some of our suggestions to make it a bit easier on your transition from single to dating schmuck. Sure, being in a relationship is the equivalent of having a bag of kittens thrown at you—but we will show you how to delicately handle that knapsack of wriggling, mewling baby cats and how to resist the urge to drown them.

TWO

FIRST CONTACT WITH AN

Alien Gender

Did you know that the "sit" in "sitcom" stands for "situation"? Meaning, of course, that characters are placed in various situations to create comedy magic. Sadly, your real life is neither "situational" nor "comedy." Ordinary lives are more akin to a boring spreadsheet of work, drinking, bad lays, and family issues; the content of these cells add up to yield minor depression and a beer gut. Not even PBS, a network notorious for airing certain British television shows that consist of dowdy housewives mopping and drinking cheap sherry, would touch this plotline.

This means that, unlike what television has tried to instill in you from your formative years, you will not meet someone while squeezing cantaloupes in the produce aisle of the supermarket. A mysterious millionaire will not walk up to you on the street and throw a jacket over a puddle for you to step on and whisk you to his private chateau in Provence. And that hooker listed in the back of the alt weekly who you call up when you're really lonely actually sports a meth addiction and six illegitimate children under the age of seven, not a heart of gold.

No, the plotline of life is much more boring and simple—so you need to take charge and be your own hero/heroine. This doesn't mean you should go up to strangers and start talking to them. Who does that? That's madness. And very, very creepy. People know not to talk to strangers—unless they're holding candy. Let's show you how to find an unsuspecting target to lure into the beat-up Dodge van of dating.

The Rules of Attraction

There have been many scientific studies on the art of attraction between the sexes. Pheromones, symmetry, and the display of good genes all come into play, just as they did for our animal ancestors. But unlike the monkeys who preceded us, we can't just bare our scrotums or hoo-has and hope for the best. We are human beings, and we have an array of subtle tools at our disposal. Here are a few to look for.

- **Googly eyes.** The very scientific term known as "googly eyes," or eye contact with your object of desire, makes the other person know you dig them. So if you catch someone looking at you, don't yell back, "What are you looking at? Do I have some crud on my face or something?" Just smile and look away bashfully. They will get the picture. However, if you do have crud on your face, go to the bathroom and wash it off.

- **Touching.** Unless you are annoyingly affectionate with everyone you come into contact with, you probably spend most of your days trying not to be touched by strangers. This is known as your personal space—and no one had better come within twelve inches of you lest you head-butt them in the face. However, when one is feeling comfortable around another human, head-butting becomes a gentle nuzzling. Gradually, you lower your shield. Your personal space shrinks to six inches, four inches, then, boom, skin-on-skin contact. This closeness takes time, patience, and a willingness to read signals. But once you find someone closing in on you, know that they are feeling comfortable and are okay with you being in their personal space. This is a clear sign they don't find you repulsive. Good for you.

- **Laughing.** We hate to break it to you, but you're probably not as funny as you think you are. So if you find yourself in conversation with a member of the opposite sex who is laughing like you're better than a *Three's Company* rerun and a gravity bong, it means that they're into you and want you to feel good about yourself. It does not mean you should hit that open mic night down at the local chuckle hut next week.

When the Laws of Attraction Become Complete Booty Anarchy

Please note the following "bad" signals and be aware of them. Although they don't mean a complete end to the flirtation, if they happen all at once, you should probably move on to work your mating game with someone else.

- **The other person ends the conversation.** This is a bad sign. But perhaps you started out on the wrong foot by talking about how you believe in ghosts, how your nipple hairs are just out of control lately, or your 9/11 conspiracy theories. Give it a few hours, mentally recenter your game, and try again.
- **The other person walks away.** Just because someone leaves you in a social situation doesn't mean they are done with you forever—if they have manners, they don't want to seem rude to other friends, guests, or people they are with. But if they don't return to finish where they left off, consider your ship abandoned.
- **No go on the phone number.** You ask for the other person's number, they say they don't give it out. Everyone gives out their number or contact information to people they like. If they don't, they don't want to ever hear from you again. Game over.
- **She maces you.** Even if you consider it the most glorious body part in the world, you really shouldn't show your scrotum to anyone upon first meeting, okay?

Single Havens

A PARTY!

You don't get it. You used to be hot shit in college. You were fooling around every weekend. You were pals with the folks at the campus health clinic thanks to your regular STD checkups. You would buy Trojans at Costco. You were sexually active—and proud of it.

But since graduation, the well has dried up faster than your cat's water dish while you're on vacation—and those Trojans expired during the first Bush administration. What gives?

You got laid back then because college was one big party. Now the life police have pulled up in their responsibility paddy wagon and levied fines on all debauchery and shenanigans. Although this is depressing, to be sure, adults don't completely stop the good times. They just change it from "partying" to "having a party." See how that works?

A party is one of the best ways to meet people. Why? Because parties have alcohol to aid conversation (unless it's a five-year-old's birthday party) and other people who, like you, probably aren't violent arsonists or sociopaths. Your friends' friends will be like your friends—meaning you can tolerate them in social situations, have semiliterate conversations with them during commercial breaks, and can text message with them when you've spotted a funny-looking midget on the street. The ability to tolerate is the mustard seed from which the giant French's mustard bottle of a relationship grows.

However, this doesn't mean you should pack your calendar

with soiree after soiree. You must choose your parties wisely. If the receptionist at the office extends an invitation to her *Shrek* get-together, do not—under any circumstances—go. Despite what you might think in the back of your head, she does not have a hot cousin. She does not have a cute neighbor who might swing by. No one is going to get naked. It's going to go exactly like the Evite said it would—they are going to sit around, watch *Shrek* all night, and eat seven-layer bean dip.

You need to hit only the parties where you're likely to find people you'd feel comfortable leaving with. If a hot person asks you to a party, it's a safe bet that other hot people will be there, too. Hot people do not invite uglies. They have a God-given right not to gaze upon people who haven't had orthodontic work. These are the parties you want to go to. Shallow as it may seem, all relationships begin with physical attraction. So you want to be where the physically attractive (and drunk) people are.

AFTER-WORK HAPPY HOUR

Everyone knows they shouldn't get too wasted with their co-workers during an impromptu get-together at the bar next to the office. But it happens anyway. All the time. In fact, the prospect of watching this happen is the motivation for most people to attend after-work functions. For some reason, all advice ever written about drinking or cavorting with coworkers is never, ever heeded. An after-work happy hour is great because you can talk about a common denominator: how much you hate your job and the people you work with.

Shared contempt might not sound like the best foundation for a relationship, but it's a pretty good one. Most relationships start out all flowers and candy and sudden outbursts into song, but the conversation in long-term relationships consists mostly of griping. By meeting someone who understands what you mean when you say "that mustached bitch in ad sales," you're actually putting yourself ahead of the game.

Discretion is the key to the workplace hookup. Sure, there are worse things than a coworker catching you midcanoodle with a temp, but most involve not fitting into your fat jeans. High-octane flirting is pretty easy to initiate when you're in a bar crowded with folks who are mostly sick of one another. Lay the innuendo on thick. When you feel the situation approaching make-out time, you have two options: One is "splitting a cab." Your coworkers will all leave with the impression that the two of you hooked up. But if you both deny it enough, boredom will force the office gossips to turn elsewhere for their nourishment. The other option is not hooking up at all. Sure, you get no nooky, but you have established a flirtatious relationship—one that can lead to shared smoke breaks, shared lunch hours, and maybe even a proper date down the line.

SPORTS LEAGUES

Yes, it seems like advice out of a *Marie Claire* magazine, but sports leagues are rife with singles. Why do they flock to these cheesy, noncontact sporting events? Because they're single and have nothing else to do. So on go the hastily silk-screened T-shirt and Champion shorts, and to the field they head with a recently purchased baseball glove/kick ball while trying to remember how to sprint.

For ladies, sports leagues are advantageous because of the high male-to-female ratio. Plus, nowhere is social Darwinism more on display than at a softball game. You'll discover quickly who the alpha males are, who the best physical specimens are, and who the ridiculous catcalling douche bags are. And you'll have the pick of the litter.

Guys, yes, the odds are not in your favor in this situation, but there is a bright side. Any woman you meet in a sports league is likely to be the kind of gal you can say "Mendoza line" in front of without being wrongly accused of making a racist joke. If she's man enough to turn a double play, she's man enough to not give you a hard time for skipping church to watch the wild card game. And really, what more do you want out of a mate?

ANYTIME YOU LOOK LIKE SHIT

There's a law of physics that goes something like, "Every time you look your worst, you will run into someone you want to look good for." (We think Foucault came up with it.) Here's the scenario: You roll out of bed with a sinus infection and an oozing zit the size of Jeremy Piven's ego on your forehead. You really don't feel like going outside, but you're out of cream for your coffee—and you need coffee.

All of your laundry is dirty so you throw on the last clean thing in your drawer—an Old Navy American flag T-shirt your aunt Peg gave you at a family Fourth of July party six years ago and a pair of sweat-stained pants. Your hair hasn't been washed in six days. You know better than to go out into the light of day looking like this, but you justify it by thinking to yourself, "No one will see me. I'll just run in the store and run in while the car idles out front . . ."

But inside, you run into *that* person. The one who got away. The one who, a few years back, you met and wanted so badly that you would have sacrificed two feet of lower intestine just to hold their hand. But somehow that person slipped through your fingers. They joined the Peace Corps and moved to New Guinea, or they wanted to give it one more shot with their ex. And now here they are, reaching for the same pint of half-and-half as you.

You will do a double take, to make sure it's them. They will do a double take because they can't believe how much you have let yourself go in such a short time. You will try to stammer a hello and curse yourself for smelling like athlete's foot, but you can't go back. Now more than ever, you know that you will never receive a hug from this person.

Or will you? Chances are that the person also lunging for that half-and-half is in desperate need of some coffee, too. Even if they're just stopping by the grocer on the way home from a society ball, they know what it is to be in such desperate need of merchandise that you're willing to leave the house looking the way you do at this moment. Now is your time to be fearless. Strike up a conversation. If the person you're talking to reciprocates in any way, you know you have a shot. So pull your hair back with a rubber band, tuck that T-shirt into your sweats, and be bold. If you fall on your face, the ice cream is at the other end of the aisle, waiting for you.

WEDDINGS

There's a reason *Wedding Crashers* wasn't called *Pottery Class Crashers*. Everyone at a wedding is dressed up to look as nice as they can manage. And everyone has sex on their minds. The groom looks at the bride and thinks, "Sex." The bride looks at the best man and thinks, "Sex." The best man looks at the father of the bride and thinks, "Sex." You won't find a better crowd of well-dressed, horny strangers outside of George Clooney's Italian villa.

Weddings also incorporate two of the hookup's best friends: booze (which, in case you hadn't noticed, we couldn't hold in higher esteem) and dancing. Can't dance? No worries. See that old lady over there, clapping her hands to the tune of "Mony Mony"? She can't dance either, but that ain't stopping her. Are you going to let yourself get punked by an old lady, or are you going to dance?

People at weddings are expected to get drunk, expected to act inappropriately on the dance floor, and expected to stumble back to a hotel room at the end of the night. Find yourself a single member of the opposite sex early in the night and focus all your attention on them. If the two of you wind up stumbling back to the hotel room together, nobody's likely to notice.

GRAD SCHOOL

There's a reason why thousands of twenty- and thirtysomethings enter graduate school each year: they have nowhere else to go. If these people had spouses—or even marginally well-functioning relationships—they wouldn't pack up their ashtrays and candlesticks and head off to places like Iowa and Buffalo and North Carolina to go into obscene debt to learn a skill that is, to the world of moneymaking people, obsolete. These people aren't interested in learning how to write literary fiction or quantify the importance of fish oil in second-century Middle Eastern society. They just want someone to love them.

Yes, grad students may sound a little desperate for attention, but there's an upside: They're smart. No stupid genes will pollute the water on which your family tree feeds. All you have to do is convince them that the master's degree in international studies they just earned is the perfect foundation on which to build a career in high finance. Grad students are also desperate. They spend most of their time in libraries and computer labs. Ask one of them to grab a drink with you, and it will be the highlight of their week. And if you're looking for a low-maintenance relationship, these are your people. They're so wrapped up in their studies, they won't have time to go out more than once a week, much less make a personal project out of trying to change every single thing about you. They already have a personal project. It's called a thesis.

DRINKING PROFESSIONALLY

Following our above advice on going where the physically attractive (and drunk) people are, we would be remiss not to teach you about their most native habitats—places where instead of being treated to a recently purchased Heineken minikeg and Fritos, you have to plunk down your already overextended credit card to buy watered-down mixed drinks and marked-up beers. Yes, we speak of our own version of a worship house: the bar. Bars have the two things you need in order to complete your path to being an unsingle person—booze and people.

Sports bars

Fellas, unless your idea of a date is going out with a group of middle-aged, overweight men who can't carry on a conversation (that's why they go to sports bars—because big plasma-screen TVs don't ask questions), we would suggest going to another bar to work on your beer gut and moobs. But, ladies, you won't find this many fanatical men in one area outside of a mosque. Almost all men love beer and sports, even the ones who don't go to sports bars, because they don't want their friends to think they are gay.

Plus, these men have credit cards—credit cards they will be more than happy to buy you a Tower of Suds with. And since you are the only woman there, these drunken animals will compete for your attention. Once you've polished off those delicious forty-eight ounces of cheap domestic beer, you'll be more than happy to dig into their fried combo platter of wings/nachos/chicken fingers/mozzarella sticks and strike up a conversation about the game. If talking sports is as foreign to you as reading the *Aeneid* in Latin, no worries. Men love to tell you the entire history of sports, as that's probably the only thing they know about outside of, oh, nothing. Nothing at all.

Martini bars

Hello, rich alcoholics! Unlike most things created in the late '90s (Tae Bo, Pokémon) martini bars have somehow stuck around. As anyone who ever drank a martini knows, the only reason God created this beverage is to get you plastered as quickly as possible (good one, God). Sadly, unlike its lower-class cousin the tequila shot, the martini requires you to act like you actually enjoy drinking it. Just remember, while you attempt to choke down fifteen dollars' worth of something that tastes like rubbing alcohol, look around to see if (1) anyone is attractive and as drunk as you, and (2) you can actually approach them to talk to them without spilling your chocotini on another patron. If that fails, try the martini bar of the 2000s—the wine bar that just opened up around the corner.

Dive bars

Dive bars attract two types of people: artists and the homeless. But how in the world can you possibly tell them apart? It's hard, as both sport dirty parkas and crazy hair, and have a tendency to yell about conspiracy theories. But artists usually shower before they drink, so let your nose lead you to flush out who might be fun to talk to.

Airport bars

There's something wonderful about airport bars. Specifically, the fact that this drink you are having right now might be your last, *ever*. This lends an air of desperation and desire to these tiny, boozy alcoves. And since you will never see the people there again, they are more than happy to talk to you. Drop your luggage, belly up to the bar, have a drink, and talk about where you are flying to. Chances are the disgruntled traveler next to you has been there and can tell you where to find another bar that isn't an airport bar. If it is an airport bar they are talking about, they might have bigger problems than having to throw away their toenail clippers before going through security.

BLIND DATES

While not exactly a place, blind dates are a place of the mind—a terrifying place of the mind. Universally panned, true blind dates are actually pretty rare. But if a friend is so dead set on hooking you up with someone they know, let them. If you hate it, you can just start acting like a lunatic, because chances are if you haven't run into this person until now, you won't run into them again.

MORE THAN A TRASHY HOOKUP

Right now, dear single, you may be thinking to yourself, "These all sound like great ways to land a trashy hookup, but so what? I've had my share of trashy hookups. I want more." Well, the doorway to matrimony is built from the gooey remains of trashy hookups. But we're not the kind to leave you hanging. We're the kind to climb up the gallows of love and cut you down before your body stops convulsing and rigor mortis sets in. That's what friends do. You, on the other hand, are going to have to land yourself a date.

If you find yourself thinking about someone you met in one of these scenarios, this means you might be attracted to them—and may want to see them again. But how?

Girls have spent most of their romantic lives being treated like shit. They sleep with men who don't call them in the morning. They want to go on a goddamn real, honest, no-fooling date. If you managed to hit it off with a woman in one of the situations we just described, you should have enough of a rapport with her to ask her out. So just ask. You don't have to do anything crazy. You don't have to plan a romantic getaway or even get flowers. Just ask if she would like to grab a meal or a beer at some point. If she says yes, get her number and call her to set it up. If she says no, well then, now you know.

And, gals—man up. If he's flirting with you, making out with you, or trying to stick his hand between bare flesh and clothing, it means he likes you. So gently, very gently, remove that hand and ask him if he'd like to see you next week. Better yet, tell him you'd like to see him next week.

The Internet: Like Real Life but Faker

Sometimes, no matter what you do, you can't meet someone. So you must do what everyone before you (well, everyone born after 1980, anyway) has done—you must go online. Yes, it's time we talked about the great singles bars of the World Wide Web: Internet dating sites. After all, sometimes people just don't appear in your life—but they do so quite easily if you have a Web browser.

Despite most efforts to the contrary, there is still a slight stigma to Internet dating. We agree that it's not the perfect scenario you've had in your head since you were old enough to determine your sexuality. People can feel ashamed to announce to their friends and family that they were desperate enough to find someone by logging on to their neighbor's wireless account—the modern-day equivalent of answering a personal ad you read in the newspaper you stole off your neighbor's driveway. But of all the things you have done in your life you should be ashamed of, turning to the Internet to build a dating life shouldn't be one of them. In fact, if you are really serious about meeting someone, the Internet is the perfect spot. Think of it as shopping for people. You can see what they do, how tall they are, if they're pleasingly plump or skinny. If they have kids or not. If they just want a quick lay or a long-term relationship. It's like Crazy Dave's House of Singles Memorial Day Crazy Crazy Crazy One Day Sale!!! And in order to participate in all of the cuh-razy discounted singles, all you need is a few credits on a dating site.

I'VE HEARD OF THIS FANTASTICAL NEW WORLD, BUT WHICH SITE IS RIGHT FOR ME?

If you're new to this whole genre of dating, it might seem like there are more dating sites than there are single people. That's because dating sites make money and anyone who knows HTML can bank on the fact that you will plop down a credit card number to find love (see: porn sites).

There's a cornucopia of niche dating sites out there for anything the mind can think of. Your height rivals that of André the

Giant's? Try www.tallpersonals.com. Love Jesus? Try www.chris tiancafe.com. Have an unfortunate case of herpes? Find others in that same itchy predicament at www.laffpersonals.com (insert joke about herpes being no laughing matter here).

Although niche sites seem like manna for those with a mean case of xenophobia, the problem with them is that they're filled with true believers from all over the country. Case in point, you log into gothicmatch.com hoping to find someone who shares your odd fascination with Marilyn Manson, but everyone there just wants to suck your blood, sacrifice kittens, and carve hearta-grams into their arms. They also live four states away. That's why it's best if you stick to the mainstream sites.

CRAIGSLIST AND EHARMONY: TWO SIDES OF ONE CREEPY COIN

Craigslist and eHarmony are the evil cousins of the online dating communities, linked thanks to their high creep factors.

Craigslist is best for finding used sofas and secondhand blend-ers. Why do you want to find a cast-off person? Although Craigs-list is free, please realize that your dignity costs *something*. Sure, maybe you like vulgar posts from people talking about their penis size with the acumen of a schizophrenic turtle ("You are the type of woman that REALLY loves a TRUE BREASTMAN!!! And you KNOW what I mean!!! You are the type of woman that shows up in a LOW-CUT top showing off the GOODS!!!"). If this attracts you, then please, go right ahead. But we're telling you, Craigslist ads are what give Internet dating the bad rep it has.

eHarmony.com—you know, the one with the annoying TV ads featuring that doctor who looks like he's just waiting for you to fall asleep so he can dump you in a bathtub full of ice and steal your kidney—will not match a man with a man or a woman with a woman, which means our gay friends cannot log in to find love. But like most other sites, it does match straight people with other straight people. If you can overlook its "heteros only, please" qualities, it might work out for you. But there's another sad thing about eHarmony that may keep it from being the most helpful dating site: It won't let you browse through profiles until the wee morning hours. EHarmony just has a computer match you with someone who, like you, has misrepresented themselves in their online profile. We live in a free, pro-choice society, so go to a site where you get to pick which awkward online dating experience you want.

THOSE ZANY NETWORKING SITES WE KEEP HEARING ABOUT

Personally, we've had luck (and so have our friends) with meeting people via MySpace and Facebook—sites skewed to a younger demographic. But those sites aren't dating sites. They're free networking sites that send you spam, friend requests from bands in Asia, and ways for you to get in touch with pals from college. The upside is that by meeting people on these sites, you know that you can have a conversation about bands and friends you have in common. They provide a less in-your-(virtual) face experience.

But the in-your-face aspect of dating-only sites is why they sometimes work. You know people are there to *date*. They don't want you to come see their country/metal band or read their blog. They don't want to sell you pills. More importantly, they don't want to be your friend. You don't need more friends. You need a date.

You need to log on to the big guns, notably Match.com and

Nerve.com. Think of Match as the Wal-Mart of Internet dating—everything you could possibly want under one big fluorescent-lit ceiling. Match is probably more popular in your nabe if you live in a nonmetropolitan area filled with normal-seeming people—you know, people who like sports, cable TV, and stuffed animals. And there's nothing wrong with that if you like that as well.

Nerve is for the indie, urban, saucy folks who like tight pants. A quick note about Nerve: it's actually run by Springstreetnetwork.com, a company that various online magazines act as affiliates for. So when you date someone you found on Nerve.com, you could have signed up through the personals page of the *Onion*, *Modern Humorist*, *Salon*, or another hot Web spot. This gives the sites a much larger pool to advertise with and saves them the expense and time of setting up their own in-house personals.

So what do you do? Well, dummy, take an afternoon and browse the big guns. See which one has the most profiles that look interesting to you—people you'd consider contacting. Then cast your lot with that site and create an online profile.

YOU IN CODE FORM

Unless you have the wit of a pre-alcoholism Dorothy Parker, making an online profile to show the world how pleasant, attractive, and sane you are is not easy—but it's not impossible either. Thankfully, online dating sites do their best to make it as simple as possible. They prod you with questions, and you reply with answers that exemplify all of your positive qualities. Spend some time writing them out, and think about what you want to say. Browse other singles. When you find a profile that makes you laugh (in a bad way) or avert your eyes, make a note not to do in yours what that person did. Make your online profile as fantastic yet truthful as possible. A good profile is peppered with humor and an earnest appreciation for your interests. It is not a place to bitch about every failed relationship you've had. If you start describing your losing streak, other people will think you're a loser and avoid you, even if they've had more craptastic relationships and apocalyptic dates than you.

Even though you might want to create an anonymous, non-identifying profile so that your snooping coworkers or exes won't find it, you will need to post flattering photos of yourself. You will get infinitely more attention with a hot shot than without one. Make sure it's recent. Unless you are a swinging Dorian Gray, you look different than you did three years ago (sad but very true). Photoshopping a zit off your face is okay, but Photoshopping two cup sizes onto your rack will only lead to disappointment and anger down the road. Also avoid photos of you hanging out in a crowd. Your friends will plot murder against you if they see them. Just post a few solo shots of yourself looking your best. Warning: the funny shots that your pals adore—the ones taken of you drinking beer out of a coffee pot at a party because the cups were dirty or taking a whiz off a mountaintop—are best left on your external hard drive. Be as upmarket as possible. Being crass or vaguely pornographic (no cleavage or shots with your shirt off and pecs flexed) in your pictures will attract the wrong kind of dating clientele. Trust us.

LOGGING IN

So you've logged on a few times now. You've checked the messages (and then quickly deleted them) from the crazed online dating vultures who oh-so-quickly swoop in to prey on tasty fresh meat such as yourself. Watch out for these predators, as they are the Internet daters who treat online sites like a full-time job. They continuously log in to bump their profile to the top, and they spend serious cash contacting every single person who isn't over the age of seventy. They enter this world armed with buckshot to fell as many as possible to finally land someone—anyone—who will contact them back. They figure that by casting their net as wide as possible, someone naive or desperate enough will finally contact them. You, however, aren't this crazed or desperate; you are selective. So you bypass all the crazies, and you spot Summersun1 buried a little bit down in the queue. Judging by those pictures, Summersun1 looks kinda normal. And look, they like Gabriel García Márquez, too! And, oh my goodness, they want to vacation in sub-Saharan Africa as well! And they think global warming is bad—just Like You Do. Yes, it's true—after looking at just two hundred words and four photos, you know that Summersun1 has joined this dating service to meet you and only you.

So what do you do? Well, you spend one of those precious credits and just fucking e-mail this prospect. Don't sit back with the false hope they will contact you first. This is a dating site. You are here to date. And as we've tried to make clear, the first step is to make contact.

With this first introduction, you will want to seem coy and quick-witted. You know what the best way to be coy is? By being coy. Don't e-mail your entire life story or joke about how lame it is to be on the site. The other person probably knows how lame it is to be on the site. You aren't being funny by pointing out the obvious. We know how hard it is to write things if you aren't the greatest wordsmith who ever lived. But you need to write in complete sentences. Spell things correctly. Be charming. Be yourself. Ask them a cute question based on their profile. People—even virtual people—love to talk about themselves, and it makes writing you back all that easier when they have something to respond to.

If you do this correctly, they will get back to you. And boom, you have a fleeting contact. If all goes well, in just a few back-and-forths, you will fool yourself into thinking you are destined to copulate and live out your golden years traveling Vietnam by bicycle with Summersun1. Thank you, Internet.

With opening up this correspondence, you have reached the enticing part of Internet dating. The wide assortment of profiles allows your imagination to roll like a Mack truck coasting downhill after mob enforcers cut the brake lines. You will spend weeks and weeks shooting semipassionate e-mails back and forth, maybe even mixing in a few late-night phone calls, until you find yourself thinking: Why rush to meet? After all, how could this not work when we finally see each other (for real) for the first time?

Here's how it doesn't work most of the time: Everyone looks good on paper. That's what résumés are for. But being able to type out a few snarky comments about last week's presidential address does not make a human being complex. Yes, it's great when you come home from a depressing night of hanging out with all of your married friends to have a sign that this still-unknown Summersun1 has e-mailed you back with a cute and adorable message and wished you a good night (as Summersun1 has been doing for weeks now). And you can fall asleep yet again feeling safe and warm knowing someone is out there for you. But you need to take this back-and-forth to the next level—you will need to meet with Summersun1. Because although you two make a fantastic e-mail team and you like having that, that doesn't mean you'll be fantastic together in the real-life version of e-mail known as "talking." If your first real-life connection moves faster than your DSL, congratulations. You and Summersun1 just won the online dating sweepstakes. But most of the time, it seems at first impression that all of those meticulously crafted exchanges were for naught. Although you loved Summersun1's astute observation about the new Radiohead album, you don't love Summersun1's choice of jeans and nervous tic. Although Summersun1 agreed with your recommendation of the new Michael Chabon, they might not be attracted to your real-life personality. In fact, although you feel in lust with them via IM, many times on first meeting, you want to run as far, far away as possible. This happens.

So cut to the chase. After you make contact and have a few good messages back and forth and think, "This isn't so bad," cut the chitchat and schedule a meeting. Trust us, you'll save a lot of time doing this. If it isn't the lovefest you dreamed about, don't despair. Yes, it sucks that you have lost Summersun1's good-night messages (and they will stop if you two discover that you have no chemistry). But the silver lining? All you have to do is sit back down at your computer, log on again, and continue ad nauseam until you meet someone whose online prowess matches their physical self.

Finishing Off

"One is the loneliest number ."

Yes, Harry Nilsson nailed it (despite Three Dog Night's best effort to crap it up) in this single, lonely line. Luckily, he took his own advice and tacked on other lyrics to create a song. And that's what we want for you, dear reader. A tack-on so you can make sense of this desperate little corrupt world of ours—and maybe a little music together. Remember: You're not looking to walk away from meeting someone thinking, "This is the one. That PhD-approved compatibility formula sure is smart." Or, "Thank you, lame kickball league, for matching me with the yin to my yang. I think I'll go shopping for things to wear on my honeymoon now." You're looking to walk away thinking, "I could see that person again." And that's what dating is—seeing that person again until you don't want to anymore. Or don't want to see anyone *else* anymore. Beautiful, ain't it?

. . . .

Quiz

Do you make a good impression when someone meets you for the first time? Let's see how you would rank in a Head & Shoulders commercial, shall we?

When you make eye contact with an attractive stranger in a bar you . . .

1. Give a warm nod of the old head, lift your glass slightly, and hold eye contact just long enough to see if the other person will do the same. If they do, you break out a noncheesy line of idle chitchat such as "Waiting for someone?" or "What are you drinking?" You ask questions but don't seem pushy, and say just enough about yourself so the other person will know you're not a psycho or secretly married.

2. Nod more than once and allow the person you're looking at to know that you're checking them out. Before they can express interest in talking to you, you lift your glass high and shout, "What's your name?" You then yell

questions from the other side of the bar while the other person smiles weakly and shouts abrupt answers back until they walk away.

3. Walk immediately over to the person, eyes fixed to some part of their anatomy that doesn't contain optic nerves. You drape an arm over the back of their chair, slur the words "Whashoo drinin'?" and then puke into their lap.

When introduced to a coworker's friend or a friend's coworker, you . . .

1. Extend a hand and ask, "What do you do for a living?" Knowing people love nothing more than to talk about their jobs, you conduct a friendly interview. Answer them nicely when they ask you questions, and they will do the same for you. You attempt to chat beyond three question-and-answer periods.

2. Shake hands, then quickly chug down everything in your glass, wipe your mouth on your sleeve, and say, "I'm gonna get another drink. Would you like one?" If the other person is staring agog at your empty glass, you hold it in front of you, laugh, and say, "Oh, that's nothing. I was a keg-stand champ back in college. Let me get you a Scotch and soda—easy on the soda, if you know what I mean."

3. Give the person a hug and say, "You have a job? Man, that must be awesome. I haven't had a job since they laid me off from the Whole Foods three months ago. You know that cheese at Whole Foods? Well, there's a guy who sits in the basement and cuts all the cheese—ha!—and I

used to be that guy. Every now and then, I would sneak a bite of cheese. One day I came into work on an empty stomach, and before I knew it I'd eaten a whole pound of blue cheese. Long story short, I shit my pants at a most inopportune time. Are they hiring at your place?"

When people meet you, they often express surprise at . . .

1. Meeting such an excellent active listener.
2. Your story about the time you won a free Saturn in that "Who can keep their hand on the car horn the longest?" contest.
3. Your surgical scars.

Your friends of the opposite sex often tell you that . . .

1. They wish they could find someone like you.
2. They wish they could find someone like you but nicer.
3. You're not allowed in their house anymore.

When attending the party of a host you are unfamiliar with, you . . .

1. Show up with a bottle of wine and ask for a tour of their home, when they have a moment. In each room, you make an admiring comment about at least one furnishing or decoration and inquire as to where it was purchased.
2. Show up with a sixer of Bud and shout, "The king is

here!" You make space for the beer in the refrigerator by removing the milk, eggs, and mayonnaise, and then greet your host with "Hey, where's the loo? I need to shit in it."

3. Show up having consumed a six-pack of Bud and immediately start screaming for someone to bring you a beer. When no one does, you start crying. You grab the person who brought you to this party and say, "Fuck you. You take me here, with these people. Look at these people! They're judging me," and scream at the crowd, "You're all judging me!" Then you cut yourself horribly when you fall through the coffee table.

When discussing religious views with someone of a different faith, you . . .

1. Frequently cite the number of world leaders, such as Pope John Paul II and Mahatma Gandhi, who made great strides in promoting religious pluralism.
2. Say that God loves people of all faiths, which makes it all the more sad that the Buddhists will end up in hell—especially since some of them are really awesome at kung fu, and you bet if they'd just believe in Jesus, they could have a really awesome ex-Buddhist kung fu tournament in heaven.
3. Blame the Jews.

Two days after meeting someone, you . . .

1. Open your e-mail to find an Evite to their twenty-eighth birthday party.

2. Open your MySpace account to find a new friend request—but notice that they have 458 friends.
3. Open your mailbox to find a deadly monitor lizard inside.

YOUR RESULTS

Mostly 1s

You are welcome at all the finest country houses and cocktail parties in the land—or you would be if you ran in those circles. Anyway, people like you well enough to hold what are known as "conversations" with you. This is good, because conversations are an important part of not being lonely as hell.

Mostly 2s

People tolerate you. Tolerance is great when it comes to racial differences and alcoholism. It's not so good when it comes to picking people up. You need to work on those social skills—and moderating the more extreme parts of your personality.

Mostly 3s

Not only are you banned from the finest country houses and cocktail parties in all the land—you're banned from the YMCA, Facebook, and most of the Laundromats in your neighborhood. Find someone you think is nice, and politely ask if they'll teach you how to be more like them and less like you. Don't punch them in the kidney when you do it.

· ·

Should you date your ex's friend?

She Says: Yes! Since your breakup, you've gone through the typical rigmarole of the dating scene—and despite your best efforts, you are still so very, very single. But last Saturday at your local bar, you ran into your ex's friend. Boy, they sure did look cute, huh? After five margaritas and a catching-up conversation, you get the sexiest drunken whisper possible in your ear: "I always thought you were too good for what's-their-name." A new number is entered into your phone. You get a text the next day.

So, what do you do? Your ex's friend, according to the Dating Creed, should be off-limits. But creeds are made to be uncreeded (unless they are the band Creed, in which case they should just be imploded, never to be heard from again). This ball is totally in play. Sure, it's going to be slightly awkward if it goes anywhere, but you're adults now (remember?). And although with every wedding season, someone gains a life partner, every single loses another potential person to "get to know." Long story short: you take what you can get.

The one good thing about dating the ex's friend is that you already know something about them. You can cut through those boring initial getting-to-know-you dates where you learn about the time they went to Taiwan and their passion for cooking deep-sea scallops. Of course, you do have a little too much insider information on them, but they're in the exact same situation. But as any Wall Street type will tell you, a little insider information can never be a bad thing—as long as you don't disclose it to too many people.

He Says: No!

When you're dating someone, their friends (the attractive ones, anyway) are like a buffet table on the other side of a velvet rope. Feel free to look, to salivate, but not to touch. When you break up with the person who introduced you to this crew, it's as if the catering staffer standing guard opened the barrier and said, "Dig in," right?

Wrong. Issues of right and wrong aside (it feels so right because it is so wrong, after all), dating an ex's friends puts you in the uncomfortable situation of being with someone who already knows too much about you. You may see this as a good thing. You don't have to tell that story about your trip to Taiwan, because they already know about it. It's like falling into the dating warp zone. "Fuck this noise," you think. "You're going straight to level five."

But level five is the part where things start to become routine and you have to rely on the foundation you built in the previous levels to keep things interesting. Not only will this person already know about your semester at sea—they'll also know which sex positions you do and don't like. Those are the things it's fun to discover together.

There's also the little problem of your ex, who will immediately defriend your new fuck pal. This may seem like a worthwhile compromise at first, but after a while, bitterness will creep in. This person gave up a BFF for you. What did you ever give up (besides your body to a circle of friends who now see you in a sluttastic light)? So when you see that ex's friend in the bar, just imagine the face of your ex on their body. Then throw a drink in that imaginary face.

THREE

THE FIRST

Date

Despite your best efforts, you are an adult. This means doing things differently than you did in your late teens/early twenties. You need to pay your credit card bill (sadly, your monthly statement is not just a bunch of numbers signifying nothing). You need to put away the posters that once adorned your college walls and replace them with bland framed art bought at discount from Crate and Barrel. You need to spend more than twenty-five bucks on a haircut. Soon you will start spending more money than you ever thought possible on jars of moisturizer. And yes, as we alluded to in the last chapter, you need to actually go on a "real" date—and we will show you how.

Dating has its upsides when compared to the lottery-style carousing of your not-so-distant college years. For one thing, it involves awesome things other than sex and Miller High Life—things like movies and food. For another, unlike your previous conquests, you can brag about having gone on a date without coming off as a sleazebag or a whore. When you walk into the office on a Monday, you can breezily tell the UPS courier or receptionist that you went on a date Saturday. Their eyes will flash with genuine interest. Why? Because someone else has judged you worth spending a precious few weekend hours on—and that makes you attractive. If you were to tell the same person that you had sex in the restroom of a Chinese restaurant Saturday, you would probably notice a subtle difference in reaction. However, in order to see the receptionist's misty, happy eye glaze appear, you need to pull off a successful date first.

Location, Location, Location

The importance of the first date should not be understated. Should it turn out to be the first of many dates and the opening chapter of a lengthy relationship that spans couplehood, marriagehood, and babyhood (a perfectly good word co-opted by Paul Reiser's perfectly awful book), it will be a landmark moment. At only one time in your life will you and your significant other be perfectly new to each other—and new people are better than old people. Years from now, when your bodies are as familiar (and exciting) to each other as a Saget-era episode of *America's Funniest Home Videos*, this date will be one of the few memories you cling to when you justify the relationship to yourself in your head.

Choosing the location of a first date is like choosing a scratchpad for a kitten. Go with something too simple and it will be ineffective. Go with something too elaborate—the dating version of a three-tiered kitty motel—and you'll get no play, just funny looks and a lot of awkward twitching. Let's look at some good and bad first-date spots.

BAD DATE: COFFEE BAR
GOOD DATE: BAR BAR

The success of the television show *Friends* was so great that it caused Hollywood observers to forget one of the most important rules in entertainment—the Shelley Long rule. No matter how charming a group of laugh track–aided B-listers comes across as, they're not movie stars. But *Friends* somehow managed to spawn a wellspring of USA Network fodder such as *The Pallbearer, Serving Sara*, and those two dozen movies with Matt LeBlanc and a baseball-playing chimp. It also convinced America that coffee is a social substitute for alcohol. It's not.

Don't get us wrong—coffee is a wonderful thing. Without coffee, we would be asleep at our desks in the morning without kidney stones happily forming inside us. Coffee, not oil, is the dark liquid that fuels our nation. When John Goodman tells us that "America runs on Dunkin'," he's not talking about the bear claws.

But coffee has a few major drawbacks as a wooing beverage. For one thing, it makes your breath stink. Also, coffee doesn't make you more attractive when the person next to you drinks it. In fact, if scientists could be bothered to excuse themselves from curing polio and inventing bells and whistles for the iPhone, they'd probably find it has the opposite effect. When your date becomes highly caffeinated, their mental acuity is increased. Suddenly, your downy upper lip, muffin-top, and tendency to preface every sentence with a muttered swear against God become pronounced. By the time you're ready for that second cup, your date will be ready to ride Juan Valdez's burro all the way to Colombia just to get away from you (and presumably, to buy cocaine).

So why not choose some other stimulating beverage? Yes, some booze affects your breath, but in a good way—so long as you don't drink it by the liter or mix it with Clamato. And your flaws? With booze, flaws are as hidden as Cameron Diaz's acne after a nice sit in the makeup chair. Not only will the physical traits you're most self-conscious about become oddly attractive as the liquor flows, you'll also become much, much funnier. (Warning: You will not become smarter. The cocktail hour is not the time to show off how much you learned about Tibetan history back in college. It is the time to show off your encyclopedic knowledge of Perez Hilton's juvenile nicknames for Hollywood stars.)

Most important, bars are just a lot more fun than coffee shops. They have jukeboxes, low lighting, and plenty of other people to suck face with should your date make a break for it out the bathroom window. Coffee shops just have the occasional poetry slam. And no one has ever hooked up at a poetry slam—not even Jennifer Aniston.

BAD DATE: LUNCH
GOOD DATE: DINNER

Look, we know your evenings are full. Tonight, for instance, you've been invited to an art opening, and then you're going to go home to unwind watching a familiar *Frasier* rerun. We get it. That David Hyde Pierce is a hoot. But you can make time for dinner. How? By saying no the next time someone asks you out to lunch.

Lunch is something you get from Quiznos, not a chance to meaningfully connect with a member of the opposite sex. When you're at lunch, you and the person you're with are on the clock. Sure, if things go fantastically well, you might get away with coming back to the office fifteen minutes late so the two of you can stand outside the T.G.I. Friday's and make goo-goo eyes at each other. But you won't be leaving together. You will go back to your respective jobs, and the memory of that electric moment when you stared longingly into each other's eyes will fade as your brain shifts its focus back to e-mail merges and office birthday cakes. By the time you get home, you won't even remember eating lunch. You'll use this lack of memory as an excuse to watch more *Frasier* and fill up on chocolate-covered popcorn. Then you will get fat and no one will love you. Because of your lunch date, you will die alone.

Okay. That's dramatic, we know. But think of it this way: Only two good dates involve food—one is dinner, the other is a very messy booty call. We don't recommend booty calls (especially those that involve eating burritos). We do, however, recommend dinner. It's delicious! You can eat steak or lobster or a steak stuffed with lobster or . . .

But wait. Before we proceed with extolling the virtues of dinner, let us advise you on one thing: Ladies and fellas alike, do not order the most expensive thing on the menu. Pick something economically feasible and pass on dessert. Girls, this will take the pressure off your man when it comes time to pick up the tab. (Oh, stop waving that copy of *The Feminine Mystique* at us. You know you want it.) Guys, this will send a subtle signal to her that says, "If you keep it reasonable, it's my treat." We're not suggesting you be cheapskates. Bruschetta is not an entrée—but penne pasta with chicken and pesto is.

With that settled, let us return to how awesome dinner is, shall we? Unlike lunch, you get to take as long as you want eating it. Also, you will not be wearing your office clothes. There shall be no polo shirts emblazoned with the company logo or power skirt-suits at the table of love. You will be dressed in clothes that say, "Hey, who knows where the night can take us?" And though your jobs will inevitably be a major topic of conversation, you're less likely to do that annoying thing where you spend forty-five minutes complaining about how your job sucks more than anyone's, ever. You will not do this, because you won't be going back to work in an hour. But if you play your cards right, you may go back to someone else's place for a little postdessert tasty cake.

BAD DATE: MOVIE

GOOD DATE: MUSEUM

Remember going to the movies in high school? It was a fantastic excuse to borrow your parents' car and suck face through *Cliffhanger*, starring a post-*Rocky* but pre-*Judge Dredd* Sylvester Stallone. Feels were copped and ticket stubs were kept as mementos. So long as you swung by each other's lockers for three minutes each day at school, it seemed like the two of you could spend ten bucks a pop to put hickeys on each other for the rest of your lives. But something awful has happened since then. You developed standards.

One of the shitty things about being an adult is that, although your sex drive is still stuck in fourth gear, you're no longer content to let just anyone put a hand down your pants. Being a grown-up involves talking, listening, and—worst of all—making eye contact. None of these things are possible in a darkened movie theater. Yes, there are some great films out there. They're directed by talented people like Wes Anderson and star talented people like Wesley Snipes. And you can watch them every night on HBO.

A date is a social activity. Watching a movie is not. And considering that the person sitting next to you is going to be really, really creeped out if you lean over and start sucking on their neck before the two of you even know each other's IM screen names, it's best to do something where talking doesn't lead to an angry woman in her fifties kicking the back of your chair every fifteen seconds.

So where can you go where talking isn't prohibited and you'll always have something to talk about? The museum. Yes, we know you haven't been to one since your fifth-grade teacher took you downtown to see a Fabergé egg (what an egg!). But chances are you live in or near a city that has a big building with a few paintings by some dead Spaniards or the bones of a long-extinct mammal inside. Go there. Point at something and say, "My niece could do better than that." Never will your ignorance on a subject be more endearing. Best of all, talking is allowed in museums, but it's not encouraged. If you run out of things to say, just walk up to the narwhal skeleton and stand with your arms crossed in front of your chest for a while. Your date will think you're considering the implications of climate change on endangered Arctic species, while you're really mulling a trip to the snack counter for a Fudgesicle.

But wait, aren't museums mostly open during the day? Yes, smarty-pants, they are—except when they're hosting extravagant balls to squeeze money out of people who look like *New Yorker* cartoons. Normies like you have to go when the sun is shining and you can look into each other's eyes, recognize a mutual attraction, and dry hump on the hood of a stranger's Ford Focus.

BAD DATE: WALKING TOUR
GOOD DATE: AN EVENING STROLL

You like history and you like walking. And when you think about it, do you really know the city that you pay an exorbitant amount of taxes to? Why not learn a little bit while spending the day walking? And why not invite your person du jour to join you?

You pick a tour that meets at 10 a.m. in front of a condemned shithole that the grandson of a guy who signed the Declaration of Independence once lived in. Your co-history buffs are a couple dozen healthy, active, somewhat older folks waiting for the tour to begin. It does, but your date is nowhere in sight. As the guide describes the architecture style of a building most people refer to as "that place next to the KFC," your date shows up, twenty-two minutes late. You cheek kiss and assure them that it's okay, really. The tour guide looks a bit consternated.

Two hours later, you and the rest of the group have stopped to enjoy a sack lunch in a park where slaves were once sold at auction. You haven't had a chance to talk much with your date because every time you try to whisper in each other's ears, you get a stern "shush!" from a woman in her early sixties wearing an NPR T-shirt and a Gilligan hat. Now you'll finally get a chance to connect. Unfortunately, your date was in such a hurry this morning that they forgot to pack a lunch. No worries—there was a KFC about a mile and a half back. At your date's urging, you wait in the park for them to return with a bucket of Original Recipe. Four hours later, they still aren't back, having ditched you to go home to bed, where they so rightfully belong on a Saturday afternoon.

So, sadly, the urban hiker shall get no lovin' (though they will know Rutherford B. Hayes once gave a speech from the exact spot where the Panda Express now sits in the mall), but that doesn't mean you shouldn't go outside. After all, everyone knows how to walk, right? So why try to get all crazy with signing up for a boring walking tour when you can just, well, walk together without a guy with a bullhorn screaming in your ear?

On a whim, call your potential date and ask if they want to go on a walk (premeditated strolls are kind of weird). As long as it's in a good part of town with some park action, an evening just walking around a neighborhood is romantic and quaint. Your date will think it's kind of neat that you find bipedalism so interesting. You can point to places and things and make strong, uninformed opinions. After a few hours, your four feet just might take you to a couch or dark corner where you can rest and talk about high real estate prices and get to know each other a bit better.

Talk the Talk

Having a relatively successful first date means you should probably stick with the typical "I'm on a date" conversation. What you should and shouldn't say depends a lot on who you're out with (for instance, if you're dating a blind person, don't ask them what they thought of last week's episode of *Heroes*.) But here are a few questions to always avoid—and a few more that are always safe.

BAD QUESTIONS FOR A FIRST DATE

- How many people have you slept with?
- Do you want kids?
- What was your last boyfriend/girlfriend like?
- How big are your nipples—silver dollar-, quarter-, nickel-size?
- Any hereditary diseases?
- What's your religion?
- What the hell are we going to do about the goddamn Mexicans?

GOOD QUESTIONS FOR A FIRST DATE

- What's your favorite book? TV show? Movie? YouTube video?
- Do you like your neighborhood?
- Where did you go to school?
- What do you do for a living?
- Have any brothers or sisters?
- Can I get you another drink?

Should he pay for dinner on the first date?

She Says: Yes!

Please pay for the first date. *Please.*

I promise I won't order the most expensive thing on the menu just to prove to you that I have classy, highly developed taste buds. You see this outfit I so meticulously put together? This outfit is for you. It cost me more than the entire top shelf of booze behind the bar there. The least you can do is treat me to this plate of gnocchi I just ordered.

Of course, I will fight you for the check so that we can go dutch. It's what we women do, thanks to this whole "equality thing" we've fought so hard for. Don't let me win. I want to know that you have a credit card that works. I want to fool myself, just this evening, into thinking that if this goes somewhere, my life will soon be full of fun, free, chatty dinners in low-lit restaurants that serve new American fusion cuisine, even though I really don't know what that "new American fusion cuisine" means.

Please buy me dinner. I want to know this is a real date. If you pay, I will know that this is legit, that you aren't just taking me out to observe my eating habits or want to use me for a job contact. Deep down, I know that if this goes anywhere, I will soon be paying my share for everything we do together so that I don't feel guilty that even though I make more than you, you constantly have to foot the bill for that second bottle of wine we just ordered.

Please pay for dinner. I've been excited about this night for a while. When you pay for dinner, I get to exclaim to my girlfriends when they ask about the evening, "He paid!" In just those two juicy words my girlfriends will seize up with jealousy because they know that this was an actual date. And not only did I get a night out of the house with a man, I also got to eat a free dinner. Every detail of this story is magnificent, thanks to you picking up the bill.

Please pay. Even if at the end of the night I realize I like you about as much as I adore the blister that is developing on my pinky toe, thanks to these heels I've squeezed myself into, I will still feel obliged to answer your phone call to vocally blow you off instead of just letting it go to voice mail. After all, you paid. You deserve my manners.

Please buy me dinner. Yes, it's sad. But after years of battling self-esteem issues and that four-year relationship with the street poet who cleaned out my bank account in my early twenties, it would just make me so happy to know that I'm worth around $50 (including tax).

Thank you. But really, you shouldn't have.

He Says: No! I cannot afford to buy you dinner. I'm not trying to say that you don't look stunning tonight, or that I'm incapable of appreciating a woman who ventures out in public in a low-cut top for my benefit. I am not an idiot. I am a man.

When I say, "I cannot afford to buy you dinner," I mean,

"I cannot afford to buy you dinner." The key word here is "afford." Let me tell you a little bit about myself.

I pursued an English degree at college, thinking this would be the best way to prepare for law school. The problem is 42 bazillion women thought the same thing. When it came time to take the LSAT, I did not make it into my target school, my secondary school, my fallback school, or the University of Phoenix (they don't even have a law school, but I applied anyway). Why? Because too many women have decided to flex their mental muscles and band together in an attempt to take over the world with their good looks, innate sensibility, and power pumps. Well, it seems to be working. But just know this: my legs would look just as good as yours if I could wear heels, thank you.

Before you look at me like I'm some sort of pathetic loser when I try to pay for my share of the meal in quarters, let me just remind you that back in the day, a man used to treat his lady to a night on the town. That's because back in the day, men made money. I don't make money. And the blame lies solely with you and your giant brain.

But back to me. Unable to attend law school, I entered an MFA program at a state university. I'm now a substitute teacher at an inner-city school, forced to shell out 80 percent of my earnings toward paying off my student loans. The other 20 percent goes to taxes. The only outlets I have left are reading my poetry on the streets and staring at your cleavage. Yes, it's rather lame that I'm asking you to pay for half this date, but don't hold that against me. It is your fault, after all.

So, are you guys hiring or what?

Go It Alone

"But what if I don't want to be alone for an extended period of time with this person I barely know?" you ask. Well, as they say in the plumbing business, "Tough shit."

Hanging out one-on-one on a first date can be intimidating. That's why Rob Reiner invented the double date (that and because *When Harry Met Sally* might have been unbearable without Bruno Kirby and Carrie Fisher there to break up the constant whining). And who knows if that stranger you asked out actually carries around toothbrushes sharpened into shivs? It's good to have a friend around to remove the weapon and stop the bleeding when things go horribly awry.

The problem is double dates and shankings work out only in romantic comedies. Group settings don't allow for the exchange of bad jokes and half-baked political views that can tell you whether you're hanging out with the One or the One You Wish Would Suddenly Fall Through a Hidden Trapdoor. Want proof? Let's role-play two scenarios.

FIFTEEN PEOPLE WALK INTO A BAR . . .

You and the gang have a group outing planned this weekend at a comfortable dive bar with a solid jukebox and a Big Buck Hunter machine. The crew includes two couples you've known since college, four single guys, four single girls, and a random who you think works at the seafood place where your roommate (the aspiring dancer) waits tables. Thinking this environment will relieve the pressure of having to come up with conversation topics all night, you invite that certain someone who you've wanted to ask out but could never find the right time to.

Seventy-five minutes into this setup, one couple is leaving early (they have to head to the farmers' market in the morning to load up on organic produce and grass-fed beef). The other couple is secluded in a far corner of the bar, engaged in a heated argument that involves heavy repetition of the phrases "your mother," "broke this week," and "that water was scalding hot, for Chrissake." Three male singles and one female have been shooting video-game elk for thirty-five minutes. One male and another single girl are making out in the bathroom. And the last two single girls have you and your "date" cornered, saying over and over about their "friend" in the bathroom, "She's not a whore, but . . ."

This conversation is alienating your date—not because of your friends' mean-girl bitchiness, but because your date has no clue who the fuck these people are talking about. Heck, your date has no fucking clue who the people talking even are.

Two hours later, the arguing couple and newly minted bathroom couple have left the premises, as has half the Big Buck Hunter crew. The other half is at the bar, doing Jäger shots. You are still listening to the mean girls whine about your friend's talent for getting tail. And your date? Left twenty minutes ago with the random from your roommate's job. You have just learned a tragic lesson: when you bring a crowd to a date, it's too easy to lose the person you're really there to see in that crowd.

When Harry met Sally (and Marie met Jess)

You work up the gumption to invite that special someone to dinner with your friends Sean and Alejandra. Sean and Alejandra

have known each other casually, through you, for years. You figure they'll be there to relieve the tension between you and your
date, because their friendship is platonic, making them ideal part-
ners for a "double date."

For dinner, you choose an Italian restaurant. After all, everyone eats pasta (except for Atkins freaks, for whom our mobbed-
up friends wisely invented the chicken cutlet). You all agree to
meet at the restaurant, but Sean and Alejandra arrive together.
Your date arrives late—by design—so you can prep your friends
on what to expect. Red wine is ordered, bread is broken, and everything is moving along nicely.

According to your plan, Sean and Alejandra were supposed to
ask question after question about your date's terribly interesting
job, upbringing, and bow-hunting hobby. They stuck to that until the appetizers arrived. Now their attention is focused on each
other. They lean toward each other, whispering and apologizing
for whispering, and occasionally touch hands. You, meanwhile,
are left asking your date over and over again about whether the
chicken cutlet is moist. It's not. It's kind of dry.

After the entrees, your date, who was just trying to make conversation, expresses an interest in dessert. But Sean and Alejandra
have expressed a greater interest in going home to have wild, passionate, porno-worthy sex. Sean leaves his credit card. "Please,"
he says, "let me pick up the tab. But could you run the card by my
apartment tomorrow? Thanks." You have no stomach for dessert.
Your date, embarrassed, tears through half a crème brûlée with
the velocity of a Saturn rocket. You leave in separate cars going
in opposite directions. You just happen to lose Sean's credit card
along the way.

Lesson learned: when you go on a date, you want the other

person's attention to be focused on you—not on whatever drama is happening with your friends, unreliable (yet lovable) poopheads that they are.

MAKING THE MOVES

We're using these scenarios to bang into your head that you need to put yourself in a position to charm this coy figure so much that they won't mind when your tongue is jammed into their mouths later on. We don't need to tell you the almighty first kiss is scary—and very, very important. Even a Casanova like Wilt Chamberlain probably had butterflies in his stomach before going in the first time he played tonsil hockey with a new conquest. But you have to make a move sooner rather than later and show that you are at least interested in swapping DNA at some point (we'll get to why later).

Putting the moves on isn't as hard as people make it out to be. It's simple—make some sort of contact with the person you are on the date with. Their hand brushing yours as you wait in line for Italian ices. The gooey eyes at them when they drop you off at the end of your night of drinking car bombs at O'Flannahannahan's. A little too long a hug than is necessary. If they seem like they don't mind these subtle advances, this is good. Some might not want to kiss on the first date—you are still a stranger, after all—but just because you don't swap spit after the first meeting, don't despair. As long as they seem down with some sort of body contact, it will happen in the near future.

So why try so hard to cement a kiss? Because if not, you will become mired in the dating purgatory called the Kinda Date, an unfortunate phenomenon that occurs when someone of the opposite sex finds your mind, but not your body, entertaining.

THE KINDA DATE

What makes the Kinda Date so tricky is that one of the two people involved (let's say it's you—because it is) likes the other and really wants to find out what kind of gum they chew. But the other person hasn't really cemented their feelings yet. They will continue to ask you to do buddy things in a torturously long sort of extended romantic interview without cementing the fact that you are indeed "dating." Think of the Kinda Date as the Supreme Court nomination hearings of dating—and you're more likely to end up like Harriet Myers than Samuel Alito.

It's confusing and awful to be stuck in the Kinda Date. They will continue to call to hang out—you willingly agree— but they never make a move. You will spend this time with them in a nether world of second-guessing, high hopes, sleepless nights wondering what gives, and the very real possibility that they will move on from watching Comedy Central with you every Tuesday to seriously dating someone they met while waiting for an oil change at Jiffy Lube. So what do you do? You throw out all the signs indicating you want to make out with the Kinda Dater (see above). If they do not respond in kind, you know where you stand. Yes, it's a bummer that you are relegated to beer-buddy status and will never be known as "my new girlfriend/boyfriend." But on the flip side, you now know that you are wasting your precious time and can go on to find someone who respects you enough to feel you up.

Finishing Off

Sun Tzu, one of the scariest motherfuckers ever, once said, "All men can see these tactics whereby I conquer, but what none can see is the strategy out of which victory is evolved."

Confusing? Hell, yeah. Let's break it down. Tactics are the methods by which you accomplish a specific task. For Sunny, this would mean crossing the enemy's border swiftly, rather than waiting for reinforcements, to exploit the element of surprise. For you, it means wearing your skinny jeans. Strategy is the broad plan for victory that incorporates a number of tactics in pursuit of the ultimate goal. Sunny's ultimate goal was to force the surrender of whatever province he was hired to conquer. Your ultimate goal is a first date that leads to a second.

Having a great first date can be a sign of good things to come—but it will work only if you put yourself in a position in which things can go well. That means using smart tactics. But a good first date also requires a deft strategy. It's not enough to just pick a good spot for a first date. You need to wear something flattering, ask insightful questions, and be on the lookout for signs that you're sinking into Kinda Date territory. Then and only then will you, like Sun Tzu, conquer the Kingdom of Love.

. . . .

Quiz

Will this first date lead to a second? Take this quiz to find out.

Plans for a second date are arranged . . .

1. Happily. You both come to a mutual agreement through several late-night phone chats on where you would like to go.
2. Through text messages, because the idea of actually talking on the phone with the person puts you in a cold sweat.
3. On the phone—but when you suggest a spot, they phlegmatically cough and say, "Sure, whatevs is the cheapest and closest to my crib." Yes, they actually say "whatevs" and refer to their home as "my crib."

Your date is dressed like . . .

1. Like they're cute! Not H & M–model cute (and really, who is?), but not too shabby. If you were in a 1930s movie, you would say they "cut a sharp figure." If anything, it looks like they put some effort into it. And thankfully, they left the tapered jeans at home, where they belong.
2. "They're okay!" you happily reassure yourself. But then you suddenly become so self-conscious about what you're wearing that you just focus on your outfit. You're suddenly very aware that despite all your efforts, you kind of look like a poorly dressed seventh-grader. The rest of the evening, you try to figure out if it would be weird to leave for a moment to dash into the mall and buy a new outfit.
3. Like Pete Doherty on a good day.

When the entrée arrives . . .

1. What? The entrée is here? Seems like you just got to the restaurant. Tee-hee!
2. Things seem to be going okay, but you get so excited about the fact that your date went to Kutz summer camp too that you choke on your beet salad and have to be Heimliched by the waiter.
3. You rush through it with the speed of a whirling dervish on a meth bender. Between the munching sounds in your ears, you realize your date is talking about some party they threw at college that would make the Duke lacrosse team look like a bunch of pussies. They think this is awesome. You think this evening is God punishing you for the time you beat your little sister with a Docksider when she was eight.

When you try to fall asleep at the end of the night, you . . .

1. Roll over and kiss your date good night.
2. Whisper a silent, fervent prayer that despite your shortcomings, your date will call you within the required three-day waiting period.
3. Lock your doors. Then go back to make sure the doors are triple locked. Spend the rest of the evening wondering if your date is outside your door, listening to you sleep.

When it's time to say good-bye you . . .

1. Gaze longingly into their eyes, purse your lips slightly closed, and lean in.

2. Somehow wind up in their car, but now your little anxiety problem is at a fever pitch. Your mind races at the various outcomes: they kiss you, they leave you, or the evening suddenly turns into a bad *Law & Order* episode and they knock you over the head and steal your wallet. You become so overwhelmed and nervous, you just reach over, open their door, say, "Okay, see ya!" way too cheerfully, and then drive off as quickly as possible. In the getaway, you kick yourself for being more awkward than a preteen going to buy a training bra with her grandmother.

3. Cough in your hand a few times, check your watch, tell them you have to give your cat an antibiotic injection, walk them to the bus stop, and leave them there to wait for the express.

You are forced by your therapist to draw a picture of the evening. You . . .

1. Write out how your name will look like paired with your date's. Then doodle hearts around it.

2. Draw a detailed grid and in each box, create step-by-step stick-figure reenactments of the night's events. With a giant arrow, point out the exact moment when you fucked it all up.

3. Cut yourself and with your own blood, finger-paint a large picture of Jesus dying on the cross.

YOUR RESULTS

Mostly 1s

The giant dating Wheel o' Love is spinning, spinning, spinning, and—wait for it—it lands on Hot First Date! With this, you win an all-expenses-paid sexy second date. Bully for you! Please walk your way to the winner's circle, where some much-anticipated dry humping will occur.

Mostly 2s

This first date could have been awesome if you weren't more skittish than a rescue kitten. Hopefully, your date will chalk it up to nerves (or better yet, will decide your twitching is adorable) and agree to a follow-up.

Mostly 3s

Uh, no. It's time to start again. Next time, just think of all the things you did on this date—starting with agreeing to go out with the person in the first place—then do the exact opposite.

FOUR

THE THIRD

Date

Is there any other date in relationship history that has the weight of the all-great third date? Why is it that we've been programmed to believe that this is *the* momentous event of a dating life? What the hell gives?

Because it is a big deal. Trust us. Fuck your one-year anniversary, the first time you meet the 'rents, the engagement party; the third date is the magical gateway to all of these other slightly painful milestones. It's akin to a callback at an audition, a presidential recount, or a governor's pardon after you got away with that triple homicide you don't remember perpetrating back in Des Moines. We're so proud of you!

One reason that everyone is justifiably fearful of the third date is that it's forever known as the Sex Date. This dating "given" makes absolutely no sense, because realistically you've only spent, oh, say, ten hours with this person, and by the eleventh hour you're supposed to feel obliged to drop your pants. Still, if all goes well, there is a very real and right possibility you are going to bang harder and longer than John Bonham's drum solo in "Moby Dick."

Why is this the "cut your losses or whip it out" event of the burgeoning relationship? Because three green appletinis is the price of admission—and the price of admission has been paid. If you have followed our advice and played your cards right, by this milestone your feelings are pretty much cemented in your psyche. You will make sure your sheets are clean, the dog poop in the corner has been picked up, and the sexy undies come out because all systems are cleared for landing for a magical stay in boomtown.

Ah, but don't check the expiration date on those LifeStyles quite yet, you frisky little sex porcupine, you. A third date has such gravitas because there's a dark side—the Darth Vader aspect of burgeoning relationships—because by the third date you can theoretically cut your losses without too much heartbreak and/or tire slashing. By the end of the night, if you're thinking that you would rather be on your couch than in the other person's naked body, it's perfectly okay to bow out of this gracefully—or as most of us do, by clearing your throat, checking the time on your cell, and making vague excuses as you walk away, deleting the number from your cell phone as soon as you are safely away from that person who will forever be known as "the close call" or "whew."

How to Act

So, darlingest, feeling an undue amount of pressure to turn in a pitch-perfect performance on the third date yet? Good. This is the time when you need to show a bit of yourself—but not too much—to your date. The two of you and your moderator, booze, have worn out the question-and-answer portion of the relationship (What do you do? What college did you go to? What kind of music do you listen to?). But now you need to delve a bit deeper into each other (your minds—*minds!*). People usually don't get naked for strangers, but they do get naked for people they know a little something about.

It's a tricky tightrope of half-truths and high-stakes negotiations to make sure you can come out on top and with your pants off. You must be sure not to give up anything too personal, but get personal enough that your date thinks he/she is getting to know the real you.

TALK ABOUT YOUR CRAZY UNCLE, BUT NOT YOUR CRAZY MOTHER

Crazy uncles are so cuh-razy! And the good thing about them is that everyone has one. Therefore, your date can relate to your story about the time your uncle got methed up, climbed naked on the roof at a family barbecue, and threatened to jump into the aboveground pool—from the roof. This is funny! You can laugh at this! This is just an *uncle*.

Be careful. Because your mind is all crazed from the beer, the excitement of the very real possibility of seeing someone naked at the end of the night and the fact that this seems to "be going somewhere," you want to share. You are tired of being locked up tighter than Scrooge McDuck's money bin. You want to tell this person you've started to feel strangely close to about the time your mom didn't change out of her bathrobe for three weeks straight or how you came home one day to find Dad number three in his pickup with the engine running and a tube coming in from the exhaust to the cab because you are feeling *comfortable*.

Do not, under any circumstance, open this door. See, the above stories are sad (especially that one about your stepdad; Jesus, you're fucked up) because they are way too personal. They're not harmless bits about some dude who did something kinda funny. See, the crazy uncle story is great because it shows your date that your family is imperfect (just like theirs), but implies—because you recognize this behavior as ridiculous—that your immediate family is somewhat stable. It's the red herring of familial stories. It's just the extended family that was infected with the crazy gene. By the grace of God, you were spared.

WHEN YOU SHOULD TELL THEM THAT YOUR MOM/DAD IS A MANIC DEPRESSIVE

Seven months—or after they beg you for the explanation as to why you continuously cried every time they went to the bathroom because you thought they were "leaving for good."

YOU ARE ALLOWED ONE GENUINE LAUGH TO ESCAPE

Some of us have insane, grating laughs, and we know this. They sound like a cross between an elderly donkey being castrated and a duck being slowly run over by a tractor while the windshield is being squeegeed. Many a time, when a prospective suitor hears your laugh the first thing they think is, "Dear God, what is that? I cannot live my entire life listening to something that sounds like Boston terriers being boiled alive." Then they dump your ass.

So, let one of your natural laughs escape—but only once—and watch their reaction. Did they make a face? Yes? Quick! Make sure you act as though you have no idea where that sound came from. Then fake-laugh the rest of the evening and year.

When you should let your original laugh shine

As the relationship progresses and the release of hormones helps to mellow the primal scream of your guffaw, you can let go more. Oddly, your significant other may find this grating personality quirk endearing.

TO BRING UP OR NOT BRING UP THE EX

It seems so obvious that you shouldn't talk about your ex on a date. Talking about an ex shows that you're actively comparing your current date to past dates, and even those with the self-esteem of Christy Turlington would hate that. This gets lumped into things that we shouldn't do—such as smoking cigarettes or watching *Brothers and Sisters*—but do anyway.

We understand that exes are harder to shake off than a half-dozen leeches stuck to your leg; they are intricately entwined in your life. So it's acceptable if they come up in conversation, but only if there is no other way out. After all, if you were involved with someone in the past, they will come up in conversation at one point; you can't just lie and say that between the years 2002 and 2004 you were stationed in the Peace Corps. (Well, actually, you could, but at one point you would have to prove it by Photoshopping yourself into pictures from *National Geographic*. It's super time-consuming. Believe us.) So, yes, you are allowed to bring up the ex if questioned, but please stick to the hard-and-fast rule of the Ex Story: never, ever bring up the pros of an ex, only the cons. Examples: They had a fat ass. They were really into anime. They thought Puerto Rico was a state. After that, never mention them again until you are firmly into coupledom and this new person is secure in their ranking.

When should you let other knowledge about your ex into the relationship?

Never—or at your seventieth birthday party, when you invite them because you would like to see them one more time before you die.

YOU KIND OF LIKE THEM (BUT NOT, LIKE, IN A PSYCHO WAY)

We are all needy people. If we didn't need things, we wouldn't have this insatiable urge to get close to someone to allay our insecurities about ourselves. We want to hear that someone likes us. That someone thinks we're not just fucked up and that we can, in just the slightest way, enrich another person's experience. And you need to reciprocate. It's okay to let the cool guy/girl act slip a bit and tell the other person that you've enjoyed getting to know them, that you think they're interesting/attractive/lovely. Do this in a cute, nice way—not in a way that will have them making a mental note to change their phone number and inquire about checking into a witness protection program. Do not blurt out, "I love you." Hell, don't even blurt out, "I like you"—it sounds too much like the other one. A little appreciation goes a long way. Tell them that you enjoy spending time with them or that you're really glad you met. They will take that little bit of information and tuck it away in the deep recesses of the mind, in a slim, dusty file labeled "Maybe I don't suck after all."

When you should let them know you kind of like them

This, the third date, is the perfect time. But the fact you feel an insatiable need to spend eternity with them or Google-stalked them before you even asked them out? Probably never.

. . . .

Quiz

Are you ready to go all the way? Take the quiz to find out.

The idea of seeing this person naked makes you . . .

1. Whip off your pants. When you are together, you visualize just where on their body their nipples lie, so you won't be surprised when you see them in the flesh.
2. Indifferent. They really aren't all that. You'd rather go to your favorite *High School Musical* fan site and gaze longingly at pictures of Zac Ephron and wonder who his stylist is, because really, those special-edition Vans he's wearing are pretty awesome.
3. Hmm. . . . You really haven't thought about it. But now that you do, you find it kind of pleasant—just like it feels when you stare at your new nature screensaver for twenty minutes.

Next time you stop by the pharmacy you . . .

1. Stock up on condoms. Afterward, you call your stockbroker to invest in latex. As your stockbroker laughs and asks if you really think you're going to get *that* much tail, you scream into the phone, "Buy, motherfucker! Buy!"
2. Grab hair clips, baby oil, hair gel, and mascara.
3. Shit. You've been meaning to stop by the drugstore to pick up some protection and some other necessities, but it just keeps slipping your mind. You're busy doing—something or other. You forget. The days just run together, you know?

You've already gotten to . . .

1. Third base. Afterward, you cuddled and made up pet names for each other.
2. Nowhere. But you have gone shopping together and consulted each other on how to match up your outfits for when you hit the club Saturday night.
3. Drunkenly made out a few times against your front door.

Your grooming habits lately have been . . .

1. Impeccable. You shower daily, practice a low-fuss skin-care regimen, and keep your body hair well landscaped.
2. Pretty easy. After all, getting ready in the morning is a breeze when you don't have that much body hair.
3. You haven't changed your razor since "the war" meant

"Afghanistan." While showering, you notice you are out of soap, so you reach out and pump some Dial from the sink or just suds up the bod with the old Pert Plus. While exiting the shower, you cut your ankle with your toenail. It bleeds.

When you make out you . . .

1. Walk funny for hours after.
2. Think about leaving and going home to work on your dance moves in front of the mirror. You've been perfecting this awesome side split and know with just a few more hours you can get it just right.
3. Think about your ex. Hey, old habits are hard to break.

When you are around this person you feel . . .

1. Totally comfortable.
2. Like you're hanging out with your old best friends: Christina, Britney, and JC!
3. Still slightly queasy.

YOUR RESULTS

Mostly 1s

Some people are born to lead men into battle. Others are born to ponder the elegant universe and unlock its mysteries. You were born to get down with this person, so hop to it already.

Mostly 2s

You're a closet homosexual, a teenage girl, or Justin Timberlake—and you won't be getting laid anytime soon (unless you really are Justin. If that's the case, why are you even reading this book?). The good news is, we bet you're very attractive, just kinda confused.

Mostly 3s

The air-traffic controller is not clearing you for landing on the aircraft carrier USS *Bootytown*. In fact, we just got your transfer orders in. You've been reassigned to the USS *Masturbator*.

The Trou Dropper's Dilemma

Letting someone know that you find them attractive will help in your bid to end up seeing their attractiveness sans clothing. But chances are the other person already has an inkling of this, and chances are they find you attractive, too. Otherwise you wouldn't be seeing as much of each other as you are. If you're both sending more signals than Sputnik, holding out until date number three could be hard. It's pretty clear that you're going to get naked soon, so why not get naked now? Why even wait to get to your apartment? There's a creepy-looking alley right around the corner, after all.

Most dating guides want to give you a rigid set of rules. They threaten that if you stray from those rules, your fragile fetus of a relationship will wither or collapse. We don't do that. We give you options, because every relationship is different. But here we have to lay down the law: do not have sex before the third date.

The first and second dates are about getting to know each other. When you visit a sushi restaurant for the first time, you don't order the blowfish. You find out if the chef can make a decent California roll before you have him prepare something that could kill you. Like poisonous fish, sex too early can scar a nascent relationship. If you get down to business before you're both confident of mutual like, the doubt you already feel will only be amplified after you get busy. Until sex happened, all you had invested in this was the cost of two movie tickets and the two bucks you spent on iTunes to buy that episode of *The Hills* you missed. But by having sex, you've invested yourself physically and emotionally in the other person. Even if they don't reject you afterward, the prospect of rejection will gnaw at you enough to throw you off your game—thus making rejection more likely.

"Wigga-wah?" you say. "But we had sex five minutes after we met. I'm doomed to die alone, without children to pay for my medical expenses." No, you're not. Sex before the third date only makes things more difficult than they need be. It doesn't make them impossible.

BUT WHAT IF I DON'T WANT TO HAVE SEX?

If you're like us, you wish you were having sex right now. We certainly do. Hell, give us a call. We're not busy. But for some people, sex is something that takes a lengthy windup. We're not talking about the wait-until-marriage crowd. If you're one of those, toss this book in the garbage and get yourself to church. They have a book there you'll love. It's called the Bible.

We're talking about people who work hard to keep their number low; who prioritize work, family, and stability; and are intimately familiar with the most recent statistics on sexually transmitted diseases. They are total lunatics. But if you're one of them, it's okay. We're here for you.

First know that your reluctance to jump in the sack is going to confuse the hell out of the other person. Shaking off signs on dates one and two is acceptable. We encourage it. But if you get an invite to come upstairs at the end of date three and turn it down, the other person isn't going to think, "All right, I'm just dealing with a highly principled individual who doesn't want to take this to a physical level until we've really connected and made a commitment to each other. That's cool." They're going to think, "I'm ugly. Fuck you for making me feel ugly."

Turning down date three sex is like separating Siamese twins. Use anything less than the most delicate approach, and you'll wind up with a lot of blood and a few internal organs on the floor. Be succinct but emphatic. No, tonight is not the night. You've had a wonderful time, the best time you've had in months. Being with this person makes you feel so good, you want to feel this way all the time. But you'd like to take it slow.

At this point, you've spared the other person's feelings, but their head is still way more fucked than their genitals: "Crappo. A prude. I am out of here." If you want to keep this person, you need to dangle the meaty prospect of future sex in front of them before kissing and parting ways. This can be best accomplished not with words, but with a cheap feel. Grab something inappropriate on the other person's body, twist, smile, and French. Yes, you've condemned them to a long night of masturbation. But you've left with your dignity (stupid dignity) and budding relationship intact.

So, assuming the previous bit doesn't apply and all has gone well, you know you're going to do it.

But when? After dinner? Before? In the bathroom between courses? We don't know, really. It is up to you, dear reader, to act like one of those satellite dishes in New Mexico that the nerdiest among us sit by, waiting for signals to come in from outer space. If you're ready to be rocked like a hurricane, be on the lookout for these signs. When they show up, you can say without fear the seven most loaded words in the English language: "You want to swing by my place?"

Your thigh is being squeezed too hard

Third dates tend to be a bit more event-oriented than first and second dates. Because you've already hit all your talking points on dates one and two, you're now ready to show each other that you are cultured, know how to have a good time, and have a few pieces of clothing in which you look attractive but not whorish, and this is how you wound up at the ballet.

The thing is, neither of you really want to be at the ballet. You know this because there is a relentless, crushing pain just above your knee. It is being caused by the hand of the person next to you. After ten minutes of this, you can't bear it any longer. You look over to your right and see that the person who seems to be trying to cut off circulation to your calf is just sitting, staring straight ahead with a glazed, happy look on their face that says, "I have a lot of things going on in my head right now, and none of them involves the action onstage." Grit your teeth and ride this out until intermission. When you both stand to stretch your legs, take the other person by the hand and silently mouth the words,

"You wanna get out of here?" Despite the hefty amount of money it costs to appear cultured these days, they do. That fifty-five dollars just bought them a ticket to something much more exciting.

There's a tongue in your mouth and a steering wheel in your backside

Dinner is going to be awesome. The restaurant is brand new, and the chef was just brought in from a fancy hotel in Vegas. The food critic in the local altweekly used the word "sumptuous" eight times in her review. And your reservation was for fifteen minutes ago.

There's a reason you parked in the back of the lot by the Dumpsters. The hand on your butt has made that clear. And though most of your meals consist of Lean Cuisines and Hot Pockets (they cancel each other out), you would much rather be here, starving and making out in the front of a Ford Taurus than inside, finally discovering what foie gras is.

But being as you're no longer fifteen, the prospect of taking this relationship to the next level as a busboy dumps two bags full of fish heads in the bin ten feet from you is somehow unsexy. Slide back over into your seat, put your shirt back on, and say, "Let's get out of here." If the other, dense as they are, wonders what about dinner, just say, "You have delivery menus, don't you?"

You're taking a romantic walk past your date's building

A walk can be a nice windup to a solid third date. But it's a little suspicious that the movie theater, restaurant, and bar you went to this evening all seemed to be in a three-block radius of a particular point. Now, as you walk off those four gin and tonics, you realize what that center was—la casa de la your date.

At this moment you're likely to be told the shocking news that your date has a cat upstairs to feed, an oven to turn off, or an elderly relative to slip some Vicodin to. You can wait down here if you like—though, just a warning, a guy got stabbed across the street right there last night. Super-ugly scene. He had three kids. Oh, you want to come upstairs? No problem. This will only take a second. There are some magazines you can look at while you wait.

Accept the invitation to come upstairs. There are worse things in this world than nightcaps and sex in a bedroom that you don't have to clean up afterward.

PREPARING FOR LIFTOFF

You have to be somewhat crazy and open to allow another person you don't really know all that well into your domain. And as we know, your domain is a sacred place of bags of clothes to be taken to Goodwill, old college term papers, and mismatched socks. But the third date is a very important one, so make sure your bedroom is somewhat clean and the pillowcases don't smell like month-old head sweat, and hide that box of porn safely under your bed. Or better yet, throw that shit out. 'Cause if this first stay in Sexyville is a satisfactory one, it looks like you're going to get a new permanent resident.

Seriously, clean your place up. Before going out on third-date night, put as much effort into preparing your home for lovemaking as you put into preparing yourself. No, you don't need to set out scented candles or replace your normal lightbulbs with red novelty lightbulbs purchased from Spencer's Gifts. This will only make you seem weird and creepy. Do the dishes. Take out the trash. Clean the toilet, the cat box, and anything else that smells like poop. Make sure that your bedroom is spotless and your bed is made. And if the only sheets you have are the *Return of the Jedi* or My Little Pony sheets you had in third grade, go to Target and get some goddamn grown-up sheets. Yes, we acknowledge the old sheets' vintage kitsch. But do you really want someone to throw themselves on top of you for the first time and look down to see your face next to Jabba the Hutt's?

WHAT TO DO IF IT DOESN'T GO SO WELL AND DESPITE ALL ODDS, YOU DON'T ATTEMPT SUICIDE

Have you heard the phrase, "Sex is like pizza. Even if it's not great, it's still pretty good"? The assholes who say this have never felt the crushing defeat of coitus gone inerectus. They also have never had Domino's.

For the past few weeks, you've hiked through the minefields of arranging dates, paying for meals you can't afford, and missing your 6 p.m. spin class, only to find a penis that quivers like baby kitten in the hand.

This is very, very, very bad. Not to put any pressure on you, but there is a good possibility that very bad first sex is an atomic bomb that will implode your fresh relationship like—well, like an atomic bomb. You get the point. If there isn't sexual chemistry, there isn't, well, much to ride on (pun heavily intended), is there? Unless you don't like the sex and are in this because this person is a Texas billionaire and about to (fingers crossed!) go gentle into that good night, you might as well just gather your belongings and get out of there as quick as your embarrassed legs will take you.

We know you're hoping this didn't work out because of nerves or first-night jitters or the fact that you both drank more than a Russian with a gift certificate to Vodka Mart. But if there is no liftoff (hell, if you don't get close to manning the rocket o' love), then things do not look good for this mission to Relationship Planet, friends.

You have to get out of this. Because, trust us, things will not get better. His flaccid penis or the fact that she gyrates like an eighty-year-old with a hip replacement will never, ever change. A wise old man (Dorothy's dad) once told us that if you see a dying baby bird who has been knocked out of a nest you shouldn't try to nurse it back to health. You should just crush it with the back of shovel. Brutal? Yes. But no amount of suckling, stroking, or body heat will get that thing to take off and soar. Like a fat goombah getting rid of an enemy, take the shovel to them over and over again and bury them deep, so they'll never be heard from again.

Okay, that's harsh. We admit it. It's hard to cut it off with someone you've gotten so far with. You touched body parts. You made it into bed together. But *it didn't work*. It's the shit Greek tragedies and that little book by that big hairy dude who became famous for writing short sentences and whose granddaughter was a mediocre actress are made of. Unless you are the spawn of Satan, you can't tell them you're abandoning ship because you find they have the sexual prowess of a eunuch. Just pretend like it didn't happen. Trust us, you are saving nights on end reading Viagra ads and looking in the back of altweeklies for sex manuals to try to see how you can fix it. You can't.

Finishing Off

If on the third date you have the constant refrain of Bad Company's "Feel Like Makin' Love" booming in your head more than your hometown classic rock station plays it during their Drive

Home Rock Block, this date shall be a blessed one. However, the 1970s blues rock group was too busy repeating their chorus (again and again) to include a refrain about if it all goes horribly awry. If that happens, we're sorry. You will just have to start again with someone you're sexually compatible with. It's better to know now than to waste even more potential boy- or girlfriend time.

• •

HE SAYS/SHE SAYS

Is liking their friends all that important?

She Says: Yes!

Now that you have entered in the sacred contract of coupledom, surprise! You have a whole new set of people to get to know and impress: their friends. Have fun!

Liking their friends is important because for the foreseeable future, you will be put in scenarios that you would much rather not partake in but have to in order to get laid without a fight at evening's end. Case in point: going to the Belgian bar to check out their friend who is playing at jazz night.

You sit at the table that is jammed full of your sweetie's friends, who are all already wasted on Hefeweizen. You are crammed next to the wannabe lesbian friend, the one who yammers your ear off about her desire to breed pit bulls. You are then introduced to the guy across the table, the one who has the tattoo of the Budweiser frog proudly displayed on his arm. Their cousin slips the lemon peel over his gums and mimics a minstrel. You are in hell. After seventy-five minutes of this, as the esoteric jazz player is still on his first song of the evening, you stand up and scream, "Oh my dear god. Sing something! I cannot take it anymore."

Thanks to your outburst, you are done-zo.

Your nail-in-the-coffin outburst would never have happened if you actually liked the people you were sitting next to—if they were people like you who you could talk with at the breaks and who might even pick up the next round. People who, like you, don't really love esoteric jazz music but tolerate it to be supportive. You can dig that.

See, these are the people who you will now be hanging out with. No matter how much you love this new fuck buddy, if once a week you are forced to tolerate a cast of characters that make Mötley Crüe groupies look impressive, you aren't going to be a happy person. So you need to force yourself to love them.

He Says: No!

There's a reason why, at the end of the rightfully forgotten late-'90s film *Two Girls and a Guy*, the chick who isn't Heather Graham leaves: because having more than two people in a relationship sucks. This is why your parents stopped loving each other when they had you. And this is why when someone tells you that when you date someone, you date their friends, you must do a Tyra Banks snap and say, "Oh hells no."

You have your own friends. You settled on them because they were the only people you could find who didn't piss you off more than half the time you were around them. Just because your boyfriend or girlfriend is usually tolerable, that doesn't mean his or her friends will be. You don't need to go to esoteric jazz night to listen to their friend play. You already have a friend in a noise band. One longstanding commitment to listen to shit live music is enough for you.

Relationships can become suffocating fast. It's important that you both have separate friends to run to when this happens. If all your friends are one, big happy cuddlebunch, who will you run to when you need to bitch about her drinking or his 90-minute bathroom routine? Not to each other—and not to each other's friends.

• •

FIVE

WE ARE IN LOVE

(Maybe)

So you have had sex. Congratulations. Even better, you've managed to have sex and not get pregnant (otherwise you'd be reading a very different book right now) or dumped (otherwise, you'd be back at the beginning of this book, retracing your steps, trying to figure out where you went wrong). You've had a little more sex and a date or two since then, and it's all gone swimmingly. You've held hands, stared silently at each other for minutes on end, and booked it home to enjoy the kind of interpersonal connectivity that married people can only recall with a fading memory.

So why so glum? Because you've been sitting at your computer with your hand on the mouse for fifteen minutes trying to decide whether to change the status field on your MySpace profile from "Single" to "In a Relationship." (While you're in there, take "Clooney-Pitt manwich" off your list of interests. It's just gross.) More than likely, one of the following scenarios, which undoubtedly show you (yes, you) are currently in a relationship, has unnerved you. Don't panic. We're here to help.

YOU FIND YOURSELF IN THEIR APARTMENT—ALONE

Leaving the movie halfway through to head home for twelve sweaty minutes of pleasure seems like a waste. To economize your time, you've decided to spend the evening in with Netflix. You've already finished the inevitable nude wrestling match and are just getting ready to finish *One Flew Over the Cuckoo's Nest* when your partner says, "If you can wait fifteen minutes, I'd like to run up to the store for some Chunky Monkey."

You say, "But I thought we just had some Chunky Monkey." You both laugh, a little falsely, but the urge for ice cream is stronger even than the urge to watch Jack Nicholson die. Before you know it, you are alone in the apartment of someone whose bare ass you know well, but whose college minor you're still not certain of.

Your first thought is to see what iPod accessories are in the apartment and steal them. But the promise of a second round (maybe on the dining room table?) is more enticing than the prospect of going home and lip-synching "Silver Springs" in the bathroom mirror while it plays on your new fancy boom box. Instead you snoop. You inspect the cabinets for booze. You rifle through pictures of family members—and then it hits you. Someday you may actually have to meet these people. Someday you may be buying this gross peach-flavored schnapps. Someday that ratty summer camp T-shirt may be in your drawer.

Do not bolt for the door. Put the iPod dock back in its proper place and sit back down. Just because someone trusts you enough to leave you alone with their cat and their collection of Springsteen LPs doesn't mean you're ready to start shopping for Chinese babies together. You see that stack of magazines on the coffee table over there? That is your lifeboat. There is an excellent article in this month's *Economist* about the terrible atrocities taking place somewhere you never spent a semester abroad. Lose yourself in the horror of someone else's life. You have only fifteen minutes until the Chunky Monkey gets here.

PET CEMETERY

You are a lover of animals—and so is your newfound lov-uh. You have bonded over shared stories of your childhood dogs' untimely ends, and even stopped by the pet store together in between sushi and a vigorous parking lot make-out session last week to play with the Akita puppy in the window. But this week your "friend" is heading home to get a first look at a new niece. Would you mind terribly, if it's not too much trouble, watching Dr. Cuddles for a few days?

Of course not, you say. Dr. Cuddles seems like a nice enough cat, and his litter box is of the self-cleaning variety. He is dropped off at your place on a Thursday morning before work. When you arrive home that evening, you discover that "doctor" is not simply a cute nickname for this cat—it's an official title. Dr. Cuddles is a surgeon, and his most recent patient is your couch. You scream and lunge for the cat, who flees to his office behind the refrigerator. Filled with the strength of a hundred Spartans, you grab the fridge on either side and pause long enough to consider whether to pull the refrigerator from the wall or push it forward and ensure that Dr. Cuddles will never kill again.

Use this moment as a reflective time. Killing the cat will not bring your couch back. Even worse, it may upset the cat's owner, who must find some redeeming quality in the animal. So let Dr. Cuddles stay behind the fridge. There are worse things than having to go to IKEA—and the cat's owner, seeing this is a potential relationship crisis, may bring a credit card. Nothing bonds a newly minted couple together like guilt.

POTTY TRAINING

Sex leads to two inevitabilities: postcoital cuddling and postcoital trips to the bathroom. As the person who just took you to Funkytown (population: 2) gets up, you roll over into the middle of the bed, thankful for more mattress to soak up your back sweat. A moment later you follow in search of a glass of water. As you walk out of the bedroom, you hear it—the sound of urine on porcelain, unmuffled by any closed door. You look up and see the body that was just moments ago wrapped around yours using its genitalia for its other natural function.

It takes a special kind of confidence to leave the bathroom door open—the confidence that comes from knowing you're in a relationship. You must resist the urge to say, "Ewwwwww," and slam the door shut.

Do not turn and sneak back into bed. Do not creep gingerly by with your hand shielding your eyes. Think of your throat, parched and raspy from all that heavy breathing and screaming God's name. It needs water—and you need to walk with pride past that open bathroom door as if nothing out of the ordinary is going on. Smile if eye contact is made, but don't make a big deal out of it. Just make a face that subtly says, "This is what you, my new boyfriend/girlfriend does, and though I may be the kind of person who finds it revolting, you will never, ever know."

YOU ARE OFFICIALLY OFF THE MARKET

One of the best parts of dating someone before you're ready to acknowledge that you're dating someone is having your current beau's roommate make passes at you. In most cases, this person is someone you'd never consider sleeping with (more than once)—a jobless "musician" who has $7,000 worth of recording equipment but no health insurance or a slightly chunky but still-cute blonde who refers to Coke Zero as "the Zero." These passes are not overt, as you both know that sex involving the two of you would only end in wrongness (sexy, sexy wrongness). Still, it's nice to know that members of the opposite sex find you attractive.

But something awful happened the other morning when you passed the roommate on the way to the bathroom. Instead of receiving a wink or a pat on the ass, you got a question. It began thusly:

"So, I've been seeing someone . . ."

You don't really hear the rest. The fact that the roommate is able to trick someone into "seeing" them boggles your mind. You, after all, have seen this person's shower. Why would anyone with the ability to leave their home without the assistance of a personal aide do so in order to spend time with them? And why are you being asked for relationship advice? After all, you're not in a relationship. Are you?

Yes, you are. Remember when this roommate half-jokingly asked if you were going to start pitching in for the wireless bill?

Remember when you saw their electricity bill on the kitchen counter accompanied by a two-page letter detailing the number of ways in which he or she has been "more than fair" regarding your frequent visits? The roommate has recognized what you fail to see: you're in a relationship. There is no sooner sign of it than when the roommate of the person you're seeing stops being nice to you. Yes, it's time to see the light. This is not a bad thing. It's a good thing. It's the reason you bought this book, to get to this point. And it would be a shame to actually read something for no good reason, wouldn't it?

The Pronoun Game: Much More Fun than the "Are We Monogamous?" Talk

Now that you're in a relationship, the most important thing is to use your mouth to express your feelings (not like that, pervert). Someone needs to utter the word "boyfriend" or "girlfriend," prefaced by the word "my." We use these words in order to establish monogamy. Because although you're *pretty sure* this person isn't still a proud and busy participant in the dating arena, you can't be certain (and safe) unless you've cemented your roles. When you play the pronoun game, you spare yourself the awkward post-coital moment of blurting out, "You aren't seeing anyone else, are you?" This question is accusatory, and the person you direct it toward will become defensive—even if they aren't seeing anyone else. There is no good outcome. They answer yes, and you're crushed. They answer no, but then they feel as though they've been tricked into being solely with you. By employing the pronoun game, it's implicit that you're monogamous, so there's no use getting people riled up by questioning their outside activity.

· ·

When You Don't Have a Choice

It's been months of relationship semibliss, but still no "boyfriend" or "girlfriend" mention takes place. "That's cool," you think. "They don't like labels." But this person needs to be taken to task, especially if you aren't donning the love glove. Because although having the "Where are we going with this relationship?" talk (a much more preferable way of saying, "You still aren't seeing that slut from Rhode Island, right?") is uncomfortable, it's not as uncomfortable as realizing that you've been foolishly duped for months and have contracted an STD so strong that even Marie Curie herself couldn't cure it.

· ·

Now that you've had your relationship epiphany, you need do some forward planning. As awkward as the words may seem coming out of your mouth for the first time, it's more awkward being on the receiving end. You see, dearest, standing next to someone while they introduce you to someone else as "my boyfriend" or "my girlfriend" is, in its own way, more horrible than having someone tell you they love you for the first time. There is no chance to respond. You can't slam the brakes on abruptly with an "I want to take this slow" or look deep into the other person's soul, say, "I've been wanting to say that to you—you're just so much braver than I am," and then cop a feel.

All you can do is smile weakly, nod even more weakly, and

then accept the limp hand of whatever coworker you're being introduced to as they say, "Oh, I didn't even know Isaac was seeing anyone." Do you want to find yourself in this situation? No. You want to make sure that, when it comes to rolling the mammoth stone of uncomfortable chitchat up the mountain of couplehood, you don't get stuck in the role of Sisyphus.

To beat them to the punch, it's time for a group outing with some people you're not very close with. Real friends won't do. They, after all, know you've been seeing someone, and they will give you endless amounts of shit the moment you drop the pronoun bomb. You need to do this in front of someone who doesn't know much about your personal life—and preferably doesn't care. Here are a few likely candidates:

COWORKERS

Normally, you're the guy or gal who has to be blackmailed into an office outing (the blackmail usually involves your behavior at the last office outing). But the same coworkers you treat like Jehovah's Witnesses when they come round your desk to tell you about happy hour at O'Flannahannahan's McPub and Grill could be your greatest allies—for one night, anyway. Next time Judy from accounting drapes her abnormally large arms over your cubicle wall and asks if you want to join "the gang" for a couple, simply say, "Sure, mind if I bring a friend?" Then e-mail your significant other: "Hey sexy. Got roped into heading to some crap bar with a bunch of douchebags from work. Can't get out of it. Wanna come along and save me from certain boredom?"

When they get there, take them by the hand, pull them straight to the largest clot of people and say, "Judy, I'd like you to meet someone . . ." Your work at O'Flannahannahan's is done.

COUSINS

Wherever you live, there's likely some relatives you barely know who your mother is constantly nagging you to visit. Now is the time to do something that will make Mom happier than a Mother's Day trip to the Sears portrait studio. Your cousin Eileen's number is somewhere in your phone (probably under "C" or "E"). Call it and mention some mediocre Italian restaurant you've been dying to try. Eileen, having been equally badgered by her mother, will accept grudgingly. Before you get off the phone, really stick it to her by saying, "If it's okay with you, I'm going to bring a friend." Eileen's voice will reach an octave only opera-trained sopranos are capable of as she says, "Sure." When you arrive, your cousin will be waiting there with a female friend or coworker deeply indebted to her. As you introduce your companion, you'll have the great satisfaction of knowing that you have accomplished your goal and made the cousin who once found a way to rhyme your name with "turd eater" feel like a failure in life.

LONG-LOST COLLEGE PALS

Back in school, you had the social reputation of the elderly man who served roast beef at the commissary—you gave it up to whoever would take it and wore a look of not-so-subtle disinterest while doing it. There are some people out there who remember you from those days. It would be good to show them that you're doing well and haven't died from terminal VD. The only hitch is that these folks might not be as compelled to hang out with you as your socially starved coworkers and put-upon cousins are. But you know the way to an old college chum's heart: free stuff. Say you have something to celebrate and offer to buy dinner or drinks. When you arrive, drop the pronoun bomb early. Your old friend will be so confused by the fact that you're in a stable relationship, they'll barely be able to talk about their band/blog/art project.

. . . .

Quiz

Are you ready to be monogamous? Think you're ready to give up side tail? Take this quiz to find out.

A former fling calls. You . . .

1. Find out what's going on in their life but regretfully decline the invite to get a drink, as you know it will devolve into drunken, hot naughtiness. Go to sleep with a heavy heart.
2. Run to the bathroom, lock the door, and whisper that you would love to see them. Of course. Just name the time and place, and you'll think of an excuse to get out of your planned date to see the latest Denzel Washington movie.
3. Grab a piece of tin foil, hold it up to the phone, and crumple it in your hand as you shout, "I can't hear you! Can you hear me?" over and over again until they hang up.

When you get your friends' wedding announcements in the mail you . . .

1. Make sure that your current sex partner can be your date. They go if they have nothing else to do.

2. Sigh. Another one bites the dust.
3. Look at it wistfully. A small voice says that you too can see your little face superimposed on a refrigerator magnet one day!

You are given the gift of a spare set of keys. You . . .

1. Slap a high five. The keys will make leaving in the middle of the night / in the a.m. much easier if you don't need to wake him or her up to lock the door behind you.
2. Swallow the bile that rises in your throat with the urgency of a Mentos dropped in a Coke bottle. Gamely accept them, then throw them in the bottom of the bag, never to be used again (unless you need to swing by your sex partner's place to take a dump).
3. Kiss them longingly so your sex partner knows how much this gift means to you. You've been wanting the keys for a while now to be able to get in to make a surprise dinner—complete with candles, Al Green music, and a little number you picked up at Frederick's of Hollywood (the classiest store at the mall, next to Spencer's Gifts).

On your weekly call, your parents inquire about your new "friend." They . . .

1. Ask if you've blown it yet.
2. Mention the one from two weeks before. Old people get so confused. You've moved on since then.

3. Ask if you would like to invite your new pal over for dinner.

You openly discuss birth control options. You . . .

1. Say that you aren't ready to give up condoms quite yet but could maybe revisit the conversation in the coming months.
2. Say, "Sorry, no glove, no love." Because it's really too soon to trust them. In reality, it's too soon to trust yourself, and you don't want to be responsible for giving someone gonorrhea.
3. Want to set fire to the condoms and throw them right out the window. You've gone together to the clinic and are ready for some hot skin-on-skin contact.

Your friends refer to this person . . .

1. By the quantifying nickname you bestowed upon them ("The Tall Cowboy," "The Art Dealer," "The Girl Who Kind of Looks Like Naomi Watts in *Mulholland Drive* if You Squint Your Eyes," etc.)
2. Nothing. They don't even know of this person's existence.
3. By their first name—which is in your friends' cell phone directories.

Mostly 1s

You are well on your way to a proper relationship—but you aren't quite there yet. You still have some wild oats to sow. Play on, playuh. But with this word of warning: things are significant enough that they will one day get more serious (i.e., they will throw at you the "I want to be monogamous" talk. You should be prepared for what to do when that line of questioning happens).

Mostly 2s

You're a real Casanova—if Casanova had died of syphilis.

Mostly 3s

It's obvious to your friends and family and everyone around you that this relationship is serious. You know it is, too. So man up, grow a pair, and play the pronoun game. Too many nascent relationships have been aborted because of the vortex that is other people's genitalia.

Ch-ch-changes

Warning: this name change from "my friend" to "my boyfriend" or "my girlfriend" comes with another vocabulary shift: what used to be known as "fooling around" with someone else now becomes "cheating."

Yes, before the great pronoun ceremony, you could legitimately go on dates with other people, make out with randoms, and keep your booty call's number on speed dial. But now, thanks to your new status, these sexy side projects are off-limits. Once you are promoted to boyfriend/girlfriend status, acting on still active side-booty is considered a very bad thing indeed. We mean it.

"But why?" you cry. "I want it all!" Then you break down in a sobbing fit just slightly less dignified than a five-year-old's temper tantrum. Such despondency is normal when you realize the delicious freedom your former oversexed brain once fed is no longer kosher. You have converted to the church of monogamy, and you'd best worship only one god.

This adjustment is especially tough because of the relationship paradox. Only when—through blood, sweat, tears, and other body fluids exchanged—you have landed yourself in a relationship will once-unattainable, sexy, nubile hotties come crawling out of the woodwork. When finally you stumble upon monogamy, you instantly become four times as attractive as you were. The single wears the stench of desperation like a sequined jacket that says "Word to your mother." As an attached person, you are infused with the confidence that comes only from nightly fellatio and the prospect of not dying alone. Other people see this, and it makes them want to fellate you, too. Do not let them.

BUT I HAVE SO MUCH LOVE TO GIVE

If this newfound responsibility is too much and you find that it's seemingly impossible for you to keep your pants on, then turn to chapter 7 for some tried-and-true breakup options. Because although breaking up with someone by this point is a hard thing to do, it's infinitely better than ending something by cheating.

It takes time to turn around the life that you were so accustomed to leading before this relationship. With the words "boyfriend" or "girlfriend," you are in a relationship. You will have to stop acting like you are single. No more will you flirt with men so they will buy you a drink, sexily grind with a coed on some sticky dance floor, or eye that hot tail that's flagging a cab on the corner (well, you can do that last one, but do so discreetly). Those acts you once performed with a fervent glee will soon become a distant memory. Oh yeah, and next time you run into one of your friends, take a good, hard, retina-searing look at them because you won't be seeing them for a long, long time.

What? You think it's possible to have a significant other while still keeping up your friendships? Oh dear, you really are new at this, aren't you?

What are friends for? Oh yeah, getting lost.

It all begins with your cell phone. Along the way, you stopped picking it up when your friends called. Not because you didn't want to talk with them, but because you were preoccupied trying out different sex positions with your unbelievably limber lover. As you drift off to sleep in your sweet postcoital cocoon, you make a brief mental note to call them back in the morning.

But when the morning comes, you try out some more new moves, followed by brunch, followed by sitting on the couch, followed by more touching of the body parts. The cell phone charger, which is over at your place, is too far away. Your phone dies. You think to yourself, "I don't need it. I'm just going to hang out with Julia/Ralph all day anyway . . ." and the voice mails from your once-dear friends begin to pile up.

This was, of course, in the early days when they still called you. Soon, you will become very lame to these people—not because of the lack of communication but because when you do talk, it's by phone, and you say things like, "Damn. It's raining? This is terrible because it seems I must have left my umbrella over at *my boyfriend's* house." Or, "Yeah, we can go to the strip club, but can I take a shower at your place afterward? I'm staying over at *my girlfriend's.*" When they do finally meet this someone you've been spending every spare moment with, it will be strange. You will show up late to dinner and make your friends add yet another chair to an already crowded table at the restaurant—the one they were waiting in line for an hour to get while you were at home seeing what fun could be had with two feet of rope and a tub of Country Crock.

Although your friends are indeed happy (yet heavily inconvenienced) to see you, this meeting is an indicator of things to come. Basically, they will never see you by yourself again. At every social function they invite you to, you will bring your beloved Snookums. Soon you will realize that you have no idea what is going on in your friends' lives—every time they tried to talk to you about their promotion or the presidential race, you were busy sucking face at the bar.

When guilt over abandoning your friends finally sets in—and it will—you will try to rectify the situation by being as passive-aggressive as possible. You'll call your friends when you know they'll be at work. You will say something into their voice mail like, "Hey, buddy. Sorry I've been so MIA. Let's catch a movie this week." But you will never follow up to make a firm plan. Continue ad nauseam.

But it's not entirely death to your old friends. Just wait until the point when they get into relationships of their own. Then it is perfectly acceptable to invite them over for a couple-sanctioned

Scrabble night. You'll all sit around, munching on hummus and pita bread, drinking organic wine from Trader Joe's, and trying to recall what life was like back when you didn't have a whole other person growing out of your hip.

OMG. Is This Heartburn or Love?

In between making out, casting gooey eyes at one another, and reading the paper in bed for months on end, you look over at this person and it hits you: Holy shitballs. Is this love?

For centuries, poets and scholars have tried to describe and classify a little thing we call love. Sophocles once said, "One word frees us of all the weight and pain in life. That word is love." On the other hand, the J. Geils Band once sang, "Love stinks, yeah yeah. Love stinks, yeah yeah." But neither of these great minds were able to describe what love feels like. We totally can. Let's just say if you have a bit of burning in your sternum (and it's not acid reflux) and your urge to touch this person is stronger than Dustin Hoffman's urge to blurt out card suits in *Rain Man*, you are in love. Fuck you, Sophocles.

There are two ways of confronting the onset of love. One, you just let the warm feelings of bliss wash over you, sit back, and wait for someone else to say to you, "I love you" (the preferred method. You don't want to make an ass out of yourself) or you say it first. Good luck with that one.

We just counseled you on ways to sneak "my boyfriend/girlfriend" into your vocabulary. But there's no sneaking around "I love you." Before we discuss how to drop that high-megaton bomb, let's go over some ways not to—because we know you're thinking of doing one of these.

- **Do not say it with flowers.** We have all the respect in the world for florists. They're wonderful craftspeople, without whom the big-white-van industry would surely collapse. And they probably smell good. But they are not the miracle workers that those FTD commercials would have you believe. Flowers are an appropriate way to say, "Congratulations on your new baby" or "Congratulations on your inheritance." They're not a good way to say, "I love you." Yes, it's nice to bring the occasional bunch of flowers home to your sweetie. It says, "I was thinking of you today." It also says, "I was thinking of you today, but not enough to worry about finding a nonperishable present I know you'd enjoy." Flowers are the free throw of love. You're looking for the clutch three-pointer from downtown.

- **Do not say it over the phone.** You might think it's cute to call your boyfriend/girlfriend up to make plans for the evening, then end the conversation with "I love you." Oh, how deliciously sneaky you are—you insufferable dumbass, you. You have just perpetrated a major head fuck on the other person in this toddling relationship. And you've ruined both your evenings. Snookums is going to be, at the very least, an awkward bowling partner tonight, because all they're going to be thinking is "Was that for real? Was that for real? Was that for real? . . ." until you finally say it again in a less stupid way—but the delicious magnitude was lost hours ago.

- **Do not say it during sex.** Hot sex can make people say stupid things. Sometimes this involves derogatory terms screamed without prior clearance. Sometimes it involves the word "mommy." But the worst offense of all is to say, "I love you" for the first time during sex. "But wait," you say. "Why wouldn't it be appropriate to express the strongest possible affection for someone at the moment when you are as connected as two people can possibly be?" Because that's not why you're saying it, dum-dum. When you say, "I love you" during sex, you're really saying, "I love what you're doing right now. Keep that up, please." It's not a real "I love you," and the other person will see it as such.

. . . .

Should you lie when they tell you they love you?

She Says: Yes!

After months of tiptoeing around the three words ("That's what I *love* about you!" or "Who *loves* ya, baby?") your boyfriend/girlfriend will finally come to the point where they will feel compelled to hold your face in their hands, look deep into your eyes, and say: "I love you."

The problem? You don't love them back. Oh, of course you really, really, really, really like them. But love? You're just not there yet. So what do you do when they say these three magic words to you that you didn't really want to hear?

You lie.

Oh, come on. Don't get on your high horse. You lie all the time. That time you told your boss that you really admired his managerial skills? Lie. The time your mom made you a quilt from all your baby blankets and asked if you loved it and you said yes? Lie. The time your best friend asked if she looked fat in those awful leather pants she bought at that Romanian flea market and you said she looked like Uma Thurman on a good day? Lie.

Of course, in this situation you could tell the truth. After all, you've convinced yourself that the best relationships are the ones based on honesty (see, you even lie to yourself). So you could say what you feel: that you could see yourself falling in love with them one day, but right now you are just in deep, deep like with them. And although you are graceful and tender, this person who just threw their heart at your feet will not understand your response. They will feel foolish. They will silently curse themselves for ever having tried to get in touch with their true feelings. Things between the two of you will be off balance for the near future. Every time you open your mouth, they will expect you to reciprocate their feelings. You just opened your mouth to express your desire for another beer. Disappointment will reign. What was once a burgeoning, happy relationship will become fraught with shakiness.

So you lie. You say, "I love you, too." They will beam. You have given them the one thing that they have wanted for so long: love. Who cares if, on your side, it's just like. There is only a one-word difference between the two, and pretty soon, the more you say "I love you!" back, the more you will start to believe it.

When and if you ever break up and they scream at you, "Did you ever really love me?" you can look back and see that maybe you did and maybe you didn't. But, hey, wasn't it pretty to think so?

He Says: No!

The four worst words in the English language are "It might be malignant." The second-worst four words are "I love you, too."

Saying "I love you, too," when someone says, "I love you" is instinct. You say it to your mom on the phone. You say it to the man who just paid you for a lap dance. You say it because the other person wants to hear it and because most of the time you mean it (hey, lap dances paid for your car).

But every time you say, "I love you, too," the other person has beaten you to the punch. "I love you" is bulletproof. No one's begging you to say it. It comes out of your mouth because you feel it in your belly and, like vomit, it has nowhere to go but up your throat. "I love you, too" isn't just a reflexive action—it's a reflexive action that *sounds* reflexive. In a new relationship, when someone says, "I love you," it means something to them and to you, whether you're ready to hear it or not. When you reply that you, as a matter of fact, love them, too, it sounds like you're saying, "Well, if I really loved you, I would have said so before, wouldn't I? But you seem like a nice enough person, and I don't want to hurt your feelings. So, what the hell, right back atcha!"

The easy way out of "I love you, too" is to hug the person who just told you they love you, kiss them, and say, "Thank you." If they seem less than convinced, be honest. "You beat me to the punch. I want the first time I say that to you, for you to get the same tingly feeling you just gave me." After all, everyone likes tingling.

"I love you, too" is meaningless. Yes, if you don't say it, things will be awkward. But as much as we'd like to tell you that you should base every decision you make on what will make life easiest, we can't. Save your "I love you" for a day when you get to say it first. If you're still together down the road, you'll have two moments to look back on and recall that you really did feel great about each other at one time, instead of one forced, flawed moment.

. . . .

So how do you say, "I love you"? By just saying it. The less pressure you put on yourself to wait for the perfect moment, the easier it will be to get the words out of your mouth. You don't want "I love you" to feel like a marriage proposal. It's just something you feel like saying. Don't do it in front of a million people. Choose an intimate casual moment—over dinner, cuddling in bed together, driving to a weekend getaway in the mountains.

Of course, there's always the chance that your "I love you" will be met with something less than a passionate "I love you, too!" If instead the person in front of you stares blankly, slaps themselves in the forehead, or poops their pants, take heart. Not everyone is ready for "I love you" at the same time. Clasp the other person's hands and say something like this:

"I'm sorry if I upset you. You don't have to say anything back, and I won't say it again if you don't want me to. I just get excited when I'm around you and wanted to let you know that in a way that meant something. But I am totally happy with where we're at right now and am not by any means trying to rush us toward anything."

If that doesn't work slip them a roofie. Remember roofies? No, you don't. That's exactly the point.

But like we said before, only one person gets to say "I love you" first in any relationship. Sometimes it's not going to be you.

So what happens if those three little words are lobbed at you and you just aren't mentally there yet to love something other than your NFL Sunday Ticket package or your new Ferragamo shoes? If your throat begins to close up, the room spins, and you imagine arachnids crawling on the ceiling, use the same tactics you used to keep yourself from bugging out when you dropped acid alone in your bedroom on a Wednesday night in high school.

Find your old Green Day poster. Hang it on the inside of your door. Let Billie Joe Armstrong talk you down until you can confront these newfound feelings with a clear, freak-free mind. Billie Joe has lived a long and interesting life. Trust his wisdom.

This person who loves you will look at you strangely and give you a slight smile; they adore your crazy antics. Although they are a bit concerned you didn't respond in kind, they will coax you back to bed where you have sex yet again. It feels really right and so much nicer than the last time you bugged out, curled up in the corner where your friends Sharpied a penis on your forehead. Maybe you could turn yourself around to this whole love thing after all? Think about it.

In Conclusion

Plato, who could philosophize circles around old Sophocles, once said, "At the touch of love, everyone becomes a poet." When you feel yourself falling in love, you begin to question every word that comes out of your mouth. That's normal but not necessary. There's a good chance the other person in your burgeoning relationship feels pretty strongly about you, too. Remember, before they met you, they were also tragically single. The single person is like a camel wandering through the sexless Sahara of life, always on the lookout for the oasis of regular tail. When they finally stumble upon it, they will probably have enough sense to stick around, drinking in the sweet, sweet nectar only semipermanent fuck buddies produce. If you're not going anywhere, they're probably not going anywhere either.

SIX

MEETING THE PARENTS:

It's Go Time!

Everyone has a family, or at least a single parent who's lived a hard life. Now that you've embedded yourself in the life of your Pookie (still using pet names, eh?) like a germ-infested splinter, get ready to—wait for it—meet the parents.

Unlike the hilarious movie of the same name, meeting the parents isn't just about cats knowing how to flush the toilet. (But how funny would that be, right?) No. This is where you find out how the person you're with will look in thirty years and whether or not you should take that job offer in Minneapolis.

Some parents are more awesome than others. Some slip you twenty dollars for gas, make your bed for you, cook your favorite dinner when you come home, and will worship you in spite of your faults, lisp, and the fact that you sometimes smell like a used jockstrap. On the other end of the spectrum, some parents should have been reported to child services—or, at the very least, animal control—back in the first Bush administration.

No matter what category your sweetie's parents fall into, there is a 94 percent chance that at one time or another, you will have to come face-to-face with the humans that once, a long time ago, spent an evening in the back of a Buick LeSabre creating the person you're now attached to. There is no need to tell you this is terrifying. However, it's manageable as long as you understand what you're up against. But remember that you must play this meeting correctly, because as the old Head & Shoulders commercial once stated, "You never get a second chance to make a first impression" or, you know, "You never get a second chance to never be known as 'that no-gooder who isn't worthy of my sweet, sweet baby child.'"

How to Plan for Conquering the Enemy

Like a ransom delivery or a Middle East peace summit, meeting the parents should be done on neutral ground. There is no need for them to come to your house. You don't need to cook. You don't need to clean. You simply need to sit in a restaurant and let them pay for everything. To help you prepare, we have some notes for you on every family member you're likely to meet—and some variations—once you finally get the nerve to put this book in the glove compartment, step out of the car, and be introduced to the fam. They're standing right there, for Chrissake.

· ·

Quick Tip

No matter how much your bf/gf bitches, moans, and occasionally burns them in effigy, you must not ever, ever say a cross word about their parents. Children are granted the God-given right to complain about their parents; it's payment for years of indentured servitude. You, however, are not. So don't even try to joke about how their father farted at the dinner table and then yelled at their mother about the meat loaf. You will come off looking like a jerkface.

· ·

MOM

This woman squeezed out the person you've been dating back when George W. Bush had every coke dealer in Texas working overtime. And you know what? She loves her child more than you do. "What?" you ask. "How can anyone love Pookie (stop it, you're making us sick) more than I do?" Let's perform a simple test.

Love is . . .

A. Emptying half a drawer so the one you love won't have
   to wear dirty underwear to work when they sleep over.
B. Elusive. You've never known it, but you've run into it a

couple times in public. You and love do that same sort of half-wave with each other that you do when you see someone you work with on the street.

C. Something you feel only for Mr. Blanket.

If you answered A, you are incorrect. Being polite to the person who's at your place only because you want sex but don't want to look at someone else's shower fungus is like, not love. If you answered B, you're also incorrect. The correct answer is C.

Mother only wants what is best for her baby, and you are not it. You could be British royalty, and when she has a moment alone with her offspring she'll say, "I don't know if you really want to be involved in that," in a way that would make Andy Rooney quiver. That's the bad news—but it's also the good news. You don't have to worry about impressing Mother, because Mother will not be impressed. Talk about your recent success at work, and she'll assume you don't have enough time to devote to her baby. Talk about your accomplishments in the arts, and she'll fall sleep that night to horrifying visions of you emptying her firstborn's bank account to buy pottery clay and video equipment.

Instead of pumping yourself up, just be as vanilla as possible. Smile a lot, laugh a lot, and ask more questions than Jim Lehrer at a presidential debate. "I bet Johnny was the cutest little boy, wasn't he?" "Cindy must have been the smartest girl in class, wasn't she?" "Anthony probably extorted more lunch money from the frail kids than all the other boys on the block combined, am I right or am I right? And could you pass the ziti?" These questions will give Mother a chance to talk ceaselessly about her favorite subject: her little bundle of joy. And the more time she spends talking, the less likely you are to say something that will get you served with the chipped glass and bent fork at dinner.

Quiz

Are you ready to introduce your boyfriend/girlfriend to your parents? Take this quiz to find out.

When you mention your boyfriend/girlfriend's name on the phone, your mother . . .

1. Inquires about their job and asks if that birthday card she sent them made it.
2. Injects a slight chill into her voice and says, "Oh, you mean the one you met at that place where they play the world music? Well, at least you've made it this long."
3. Acts as if you haven't been talking and says, "Your father's been having digestive problems again. I made an appointment for him to see the doctor, but he refuses to go. Maybe you can talk some sense into him."

When your significant other asks what you're doing online and you say, "Looking at ticket prices to go home," he or she . . .

1. Asks when you were planning to go and says, "You know, I have some vacation days saved up, and I've always wanted to see Ohio."
2. Complains about the cost of airfare and the emptiness of their bank account. Not that a free trip wouldn't be great. It's just so expensive, you know?
3. Says, "Why would you want to go home when every-

thing you need is right here?" then "accidentally" unplugs the surge protector that the computer is hooked up to. As the machine reboots, you're asked if you'd mind getting off it for a moment. There's this really hilarious Tyra Banks clip on YouTube.

In the past, when you've brought dates home, your family reacted by . . .

1. Gathering together for a nice family meal. Mom cooks a traditional dish from the old country, and Dad proudly tells the story about the time you placed second at the county spelling bee. You were totally robbed on "cephalalgia."
2. Fixing up a museum-quality replica of the room you slept in as a twelve-year-old—and fixing up the sofa bed in the den for your date.
3. Insisting that your dad has always had a "no shorts at the dinner table" rule. Maybe you'd remember these things if you visited home a little more often.

When your boyfriend/girlfriend says they would like to meet your family, you . . .

1. Call your mom and say, "I'm coming home—and I'm bringing the bestest surprise ever."
2. Stare blankly ahead as you have an acid-worthy flashback about every embarrassing thing your parents ever did to you in front of other people. Highlights include the time your mom was thrown out of your school performance

of "You're a Good Man, Charlie Brown" for heckling the kid who played Linus and the time you brought your friend home for a sleepover, only to find your dad in the living room, wearing only a towel, creepily watching *SportsCenter*. You snap out of your coma and in the most resigned voice you can manage, say, "It's your funeral."

3. Raise your finger to your temple and make a motion as if you are shooting yourself in the head with a gun. When you find yourself still alive, you have a small panic attack, then go out to buy yourself a real gun. Stupid waiting period.

On your most recent trip home, your mother . . .

1. Insists on speaking with your boyfriend or girlfriend on the phone when you call them after dinner. You protest, but she gets her way and the two of them hit it off. After an hour and a half of conversation, she hands the phone back to you with a smug look.

2. Asks why you never bring anyone with you. What about that nice person you've been seeing? Are you still together? She then promises that if you would just not treat her as though you are ashamed of her, she would start taking her medication again.

3. Spends the entire time smoking weed and trying to teach herself how to play "(Don't Fear) The Reaper" on the ukulele. At one point she rides off on a motorcycle with a guy named Harvard. You suspect he is unaffiliated with the university of the same name. They go missing for three days.

Mostly 1s

Home is where the heart is, and it's where you should be headed with your newfound playmate in tow. Yes, you'll face the usual stresses, but they will be just that—usual. It'll be nothing like what your friend with the alcoholic mother and the gay father had to go through.

Mostly 2s

It's safe to bring someone home, but physical security is pretty much all you can promise. They will not be shot, burned, or stabbed in the face—but the emotional damage inflicted could be just as severe.

Mostly 3s

Just pretend you don't have a family. It'll save you airfare, anyway.

• •

VARIANTS

Alcoholic Mom

Alternative names: Mrs. Robinson, Sherry Sally, "Don't answer that cell phone call."

Beware Alcoholic Mom! Although she appears to be the epitome of maternal bliss by daylight, by night she's groping you, calling your cell number, and threatening to get in the car to go buy Virginia Slims even if she has the blood-alcohol level of a blonde socialite.

How to deal: With caution and early in the day. But know the great thing about Alcoholic Mom (besides the well-stocked liquor cabinet) is that every morning it's tabula rasa. The night before when you had five too many and starting spouting off the virtues of communism and your ex-girlfriends' tattoos at the dinner table? All will be forgotten by the morning because she *wants* to forget as well. Years of gin drinking have erased all memory function. So as long as you act as though everything is all fine and dandy—even if the night before dissolved into a Freudian nightmare—so will she.

Jesus-Freak Mom

Alternative names: The Virgin Mary, la Virgen de Guadalupe, Bride of Christenstein.

In Jesus-Freak Mom's house, you won't have to endure any of the awkward shouting that you would, say, at Passover after the fourth cup of wine. What you will have to endure is a lot of backhanded compliments and tsk-tsking. You see, Jesus-Freak Mom disapproves of the fact that your existence proves your parents once fornicated. You're starting out at a deficit.

How to deal: Unless you were catechized enough as a child to know what a catechism is, don't even try to engage Jesus-Freak Mom in religious conversation. Yeah, you know that one Bible verse about stoning someone to death should they plant unlike crops side by side—you break it out all the time whenever you catch someone on TV talking about the Bible condemning homosexuality. Keep it to yourself. Not only will you get schooled hard by Jesus-Freak Mom, but you may as well wear a T-shirt that says, "My Jewish/Islamist/Satanist parents never made me read the Bible, and I love fags." Instead, keep a low profile. Nod with hints of concern and approval whenever she mentions the Lord. When she finally gets around to asking you about your faith, dodge the bullet by asking if she knows of any churches in the area friendly to young couples—young couples like yourself and her child.

Successful Mom

Alternative names: Leona Helmsley, Martha Stewart, Rupert Murdoch with a vagina.

There is nothing we love more than a strong, successful woman. And there's nothing we hate more than dating her child. Why? Because finding out your significant other's mom is an Ivy-educated, six-figure, buttoned-down alpha woman is like holding up a 7-Eleven with a fake gun and seeing Batman's shadow pass across the Slurpee machine. No matter what you do, you're screwed. Your opponent is smarter than you, stronger than you, and has an endless supply of very expensive gadgets to baffle you with.

How to deal: You have to prove you can play in this woman's league or you're sunk. Play offense, hard-core. You must exude confidence while talking about your work and your education— no matter how limited. But you must also make sure not to sound like you're trying too hard. Successful Mom can spot bullshit from a mile away. So don't lie. Just do as the song says: "Accentuate the positive. Eliminate the negative."

DAD

Though also invested in the well-being of the person who dragged you into this mess, Dad, it is important to remember, never squeezed anything more impressive than a kidney stone out of his privates. Sure, he wants what's best for his kids, but really he just wants some goddamn peace and quiet. Happiness is a bonus and probably not one he has much experience with.

Yes, he's slaved his whole life to provide, but now that the kids have finally moved out, he's more concerned with having some privacy each day to collect his thoughts and get massage-parlor hand jobs. Your visit isn't the event of the month, as it is for Mom. It's just something to get in the way of his weekly appointment with Svetlana.

Which is not to imply that dealing with Dad is a no-pressure situation. Girls, he knows just by looking at you how many guys you slept with in college. Guys, he knows just by looking at you how many guys *you* slept with in college, too.

While cozying up to Mom is not an option, getting into Dad's good graces isn't quite as hard as getting airside at JFK without a boarding pass. And, girls, it won't involve "accidentally" grazing his cheek with your breasts as you make your way to your seat at dinner (not that it would kill you to do so). The path to his heart is surprisingly gender neutral. Here are some talking points:

- **Politics.** Trying to mimic your father-in-like's political views is a mission with about as much potential for success as Eddie Murphy in a fat suit. He knows a poser when he sees one. If the two of you are on opposite sides of the aisle, don't pretend—just think of one or two issues that you can stomach crossing party lines on for one evening. Dad's a conservative and you're a liberal? Tell him you can see the wisdom in a flat-tax system. He's a liberal and you're conservative? Mention you rather like the taste of granola. You will bond over these issues, and it will be years, if ever, before he realizes you were lying through your teeth.
- **Sports.** Find out who his favorite team is, then express a passing interest in their greatest rival. Don't know sports?

Don't worry. The point of this exercise is to allow Dad
to spend hours explaining to you why the Yankees are
better than the Red Sox or why Rex Grossman couldn't
hold Brett Favre's jock. The less you know, the more fun
Dad will have hammering away at you—and after all that
hammering, he'll feel something like pity for you.

- **Career.** Unless you're dating Prince William, Dad has
spent his whole life working. He has a lifetime's worth
of stories about times when he was underappreciated,
times when he single-handedly saved his employer's ass,
and times when some guy did something totally crazy at
a conference in Jacksonville—and he's dying for someone, anyone, to listen to them. You'll do. Just take a deep
breath, open your mouth, and say, "So, sir, what do you
do for a living?" Then have a cup of coffee. You're gonna
need it.

VARIANTS

Supermasculine Dad
Alternative names: Papa Angry, Muscle Man, the Killer
Supermasculine Dad, if he felt like it, could kill you with one
fell swoop of his giant bear-paw hand. Gentlemen, Supermasculine Dad will make you cut the grass, make him a margarita, and
do fifty push-ups—all within the first ten minutes of being introduced. Ladies—well, he's going to spend a long time looking at
your tits.

How to deal: Sadly, it is almost impossible for another male
to impress Supermasculine Dad, unless you've been a marine and
rescued six of your war buddies while liberating Iraq (and none
of them better have been Navy guys, goddamnit). The best thing

you can do is swallow whatever pebble-size bit of masculinity you do have and let him know, telepathically, that though you are screwing his daughter, you're really, really sorry about it and you will never, ever challenge him for the role of dominant male. Girls, remember that thing with your breasts and his cheek we just told you that you wouldn't have to do? Do it.

Burnout Dad

Alternative names: The Rug, What's-his-name? Mr. Nobody.

Poor Burnout Dad; at the age of fifty-five, he's dead to the world. A life of being buried by spreadsheets, a bitter wife who stopped having sex with him years ago, that extra twenty pounds around his midsection and nothing to show for it but a house at the end of a cul de sac in Ohio (America's own cul de sac) has made Burnout Dad a fleshy mass of disappointment.

How to deal: Does it really matter? Burnout Dad will like you or he won't. He has no opinion on anything—he stopped feeling in 1985.

Nerd-Alert Dad

Alternative names: Poindexter, Mr. Wizard, NPR Listener-Contributor.

Chances are Nerd-Alert Dad will like you. He likes most people. But not many people like Nerd-Alert Dad. He's poorly socialized, full to bursting with useless information, and couldn't tell a decent story to save the life of a *National Geographic* photographer. Nerd-Alert Dad will try to talk you to death from the moment you shake hands. The hard part will be keeping yourself from steak-knifing him to death before the evening is through.

How to deal: Suck it up. Yes, Nerd-Alert Dad is superboring and supertalkative, and you can't stop thinking about giving him a wedgie, but you must maintain control. The best way to make an ally of Nerd-Alert Dad—and you need all the allies you can get—is to not just nod your head as he explains how an electron microscope works. Everyone does this to him. He'll know he's being patronized. Actually ask questions of Nerd-Alert Dad: "So, does the electron microscope work like a regular microscope?" "What's an electron?" "Have you always been this smart?" Before you know it, Nerd-Alert Dad will be making you a peanut butter sandwich—and explaining red shift to you.

TWO PARENTS AS ONE: PERFECT MOM AND DAD

Alternative names: The Disgusting Ones, Parents Awesome, The Ones to Look Up To.

Although one might feel slightly nervous when meeting the perfect mom and dad—the couple that has somehow remained happy, well-adjusted, and beautiful even through the Nixon administration—you shouldn't worry. Sure, you'll have nothing in common with them but even if Perfect Mom and Dad hate the very ground you walk on, they will never say a cross word against you. Only people with personality flaws gossip. They will only whisper their concerns to each other late at night while trying to get some sleep on their perfectly made bed.

How to approach: You don't need to approach with excellence like this; just sit back and enjoy the perfection. They are there to make everything okay.

OLDER SISTER OR BROTHER

Nicknames: Brohan, Sis, Joan Cusack.
While Mom and Dad may cut the most imposing figures at the

dinner table, older siblings pose the greatest threat to your goal of escaping your visit without permanent emotional scarring or a derisive nickname uttered only behind your back. Older siblings know everything about the person you're with that your parents don't. They're the ones who drove across town in the middle of the night when your sweetie's shitball friends abandoned them at a party. They're the ones who ponied up for bond after the weed bust. They also know about you. Because they don't spend hours each day imagining the perfect person for their junior sibling to spend a lifetime with, they tend to get more info about the not-quite-perfect person you are, thanks to them being the go-to person when things get rough in your relationship. Think no one at the dinner table knows you made out with some random at a party between dates two and three? Think again.

There are two kinds of older siblings: Those with families of their own and those without. Those with will judge you by the same criteria that Mom and Dad will use (Are you good breeding stock? Can your credit card debt be consolidated?) but more harshly. Most likely, they are just reaching the point in their own marriage where flaws that were once overlooked have become fissures, and those fissures have been sealed up by children and turned into scars of resentment. Unlike Mom and Dad, who remember early marriage only as a time when they could still look each other in the eyes, the older sibling is living the nightmare of the young and the married. Every potential problem you pose is like fecal matter under the black light of their disapproving gaze.

How to approach: With drink firmly in hand and a knowing wink about the parents-in-law's love of Longaberger baskets. The married brother or sister loves inside jokes—as well as anything that isn't a reminder of how boring they've become. If they have children, you're golden. Children are the great weakness of married siblings. Parents of real children—not fake, grown-up children—are willing to afford countless free passes to anyone who clearly has no interest in kidnapping their child. The smart dater comes prepared with toys—and not toys kids will enjoy, like Metroid video games or Bratz dolls. Get over to the Discovery Channel store and buy some boring, educational crap with a picture of a whale or some simple math on the front of the box. The kid will hate you (rightfully), but the kid's parent will think you've got what it takes to raise a child who won't be a bad influence on their kids.

Single older siblings are equally vulnerable. No, they have no immediate family to use as human chess pieces, but they do have a deep, aching desire to not be single anymore—especially now that their younger sibling is seeing someone. Simply dangle your attractive friends and coworkers as bait. Sure, you may eventually have to facilitate some awkward, ill-fated meeting, but that's what friends are for—to be your pawns.

YOUNGER SISTER OR BROTHER

Alternative names: The Kid, The Good One, The Accident.

On the surface, younger siblings pose no danger. They have less interest in their sibling's life than the clerk at his or her deli does (a deli needs patrons, after all). A high school- or college-age human being is too busy discovering the effects of Vicodin mixed with weed mixed with beer mixed with oral stimulation to worry about whatever the hell it is you're doing to his or her sibling.

How to approach: Don't be fooled. A younger sibling is the most unstable element at the dinner table. Say, for instance, you express an affection for the music of Interpol. You will quickly learn that your opinion is not merely wrong, it's "total fucking bullshit." That opinion will be expressed loudly and in front of the entire family. The younger sibling, incensed by your lack of taste, will grill you loudly on every band, movie, and TV show (no books, don't worry) that you like and piss on all of them. This will continue, over the protests of Dad, who just wants his goddamn peace and quiet, until the hellspawn finally tricks you into saying you like the work of a film director who was recently arrested for rape or drug possession. Game over. So how do you navigate such a minefield? With unconditional love. Nothing disarms a self-absorbed young person conditioned to being tuned out more than the appearance of genuine interest in their life. Just make sure you don't look like you love the baby sister or brother *too* much. Hey, we're not accusing you of anything but, well, you know. You can't be too careful, right? With that whole *To Catch a Predator* nonsense, every parent is doing background checks on everyone within a twenty-mile radius. That's all we're saying. Just don't be creepy, okay?

A GOOD SOLDIER BRINGS EQUIPMENT INTO THE FIELD

Gifts

When meeting the parents, come with a bribe firmly in hand. These bribes—known to wedding attendees and Santa's elves as "gifts"—will impress the family enough to overlook the fact that you didn't bother to take your shirt in to be dry-cleaned before the big meeting. These bribes can take many forms, but we suggest erring on the side of ordinary. A box of Godiva chocolates; a salad bowl; a recipe book. Barnes & Noble probably has a display table that reads, "Impress the folks weekend!" somewhere within their cavernous (yet disarmingly cozy) warehouse of books. Just walk in and buy the most impersonal thing you see with flowers or a leather binding on it. This is the good stuff—the black-tar heroin of parental gifting. But ultimately, whether they love or hate your offering, it's the thought (and especially the ability to follow through with this thought) that counts.

Manners

No worries if you aren't trained in the ways of Emily Post. Manners are easy to fake. How? Just say "ma'am" and "sir" a lot, and open doors for them. The 'rents will overlook the fact that you used a knife to stir your drink at the dinner table and threw that spilled salt over your shoulder into the next table over's entrée.

How will you make them overlook, you ask? By the simple act of sending a thank-you note. In the land of Evites and our old friend electronic mail, we understand that the only stationery you own is from 1983 and emblazoned with Snoopy characters. However, it's important to write a note after important occasions. Parents *love* thank-you notes. You don't need to be Faulkner. You don't even need to have good penmanship. You just need to find an appropriate piece of stationery (i.e., not the back of your cigarette pack) to write "Thank you for treating _____ and me to that lovely dinner last Friday night. The Bloomin' Onion was yummy, and the company even better. Hope to see you soon." That's it. Sure, it's torturous to follow through with all the steps—the finding of the stamps, the finding of the address, the finding of an actual mailbox—but it's worth it. With a simple thank-you note, the others before you will be forgotten instantly. Except for the one who went to an Ivy League school. That bitch will be forever ingrained in their memories.

Should you tell their parents about your first marriage?

He Says: Yes!

Sometimes life proceeds at a *Gilmore Girls*–esque pace. You go to high school, get good grades, land at an Ivy League school, take some time off to discover yourself and get your shit back together in time to graduate with a decent GPA, then land a job with some upward mobility.

And sometimes you get married and divorced before the age of thirty-two.

Now that you've been through the counseling, the lawyer fees, and the divvying up of wedding gifts, you realize that all your groomsmen were right when they whispered to you as she walked down the aisle, "Dude, you are making a huge mistake." It *was* a mistake. You are a divorcé. But this doesn't mean the rest of your life is doomed. You know that it's difficult to tell someone you're interested in that you were once someone else's husband or wife. It's even harder to tell their parents.

The good news is, being familiar with the divorce process, you're no stranger to hard. Life is hard. And you have no reason to be ashamed of your past decisions, even if you are a bit embarrassed that you now understand she was a lesbian *the whole time*. When you meet your new love interest's folks, be straightforward about your past. You don't have to volunteer unsolicited information, but you also don't have to lie or talk around big chunks of your personal history (unless they involve a love of the Insane Clown Posse). Simply be honest and follow the rules of decorum for meeting someone else's family. Even if they have a less than ideal reaction, at least they know you don't have a problem with commitment.

She Says: No! You were young, foolish, and your boyfriend really needed that green card. Hey, it was easier than breaking up and trying to do the long-distance thing from Uruguay. Little did you know that in two years, once he established residency, things would fall apart at such a fast clip.

But now you are older, wiser, and make sure you get into relationships that actually go somewhere.

So what do you do about your dalliance when you meet your latest flame's parents? You just keep your mouth shut. This is an introductory period to these new people. The time when you are charming and politely laugh at their stories about what your Pookie was like as a baby. You don't need to disclose every aspect of your past. If you had a bad tattoo that you got at Lollapalooza in 1999, would you on first meeting these people show it off to them with an apologetic slap to your forehead? No, you would keep that shit hidden.

Once the relationship progresses and these people become more familiar with your character, it should be up to Pookie to tell his parents about that pesky first marriage, if he so chooses. By this time, they will have grown attached to you and will be able to look past some of your past bad decisions. They still might shudder at your yin-yang tat, however.

. . . .

DESPITE ALL OF THIS, THEY HATE YOU

We're sorry, friend, we know you tried. But many times, parents will just hate you. The reasons are many, and we won't get into them. Okay, you twisted our arm. Your religion, your skin color, or the fact that you're "technically not a man or a woman" isn't helping matters. Not to get all serious on you, but we will. Prejudices are almost impossible to overcome. You can convert to their faith, get a skin bleaching cream, but it will all be for naught. Bigoted parents will never change their stripes—even if you try to. This is a very sad situation to be in, and we feel awful for you. But remember that, though having a good relationship with the 'rents can make life easier, you're in this relationship with one other person—not three people. Talk to your mate about what they feel. It's okay for his or her parents to hate you. What's not okay is for the other person to resent you for not getting along with their parents. Your partner needs to be on your side 100 percent—even if that means risking alienation from the two ignorant people who happened to raise him or her. You can't head into a successful committed relationship with this kind of baggage. You'll have plenty of opportunity to pick up other baggage of your own making later.

Finishing Off

The Fresh Prince once said, "Take it from me: parents just don't understand." So don't think of it as meeting the parents. Think of it as meeting two old people who will buy you dinner. The fact that their child showed enough promise to actually develop a relationship with another human being will please them; the fact that you can read and understand English will doubly please them. Just treat them with respect, no matter how crazy they are, and all should be kosher. Oh, and seriously, don't have sex with either of them. That's a big ol' no-no.

. . . .

Happy (and Not-So-Happy) Holidays

Much of the meeting of parents in America happens over holiday weekends. This makes perfect sense. A three-day weekend, after all, is much better spent getting reacquainted with family members' ailments and complaints than doing something relaxing and enjoyable. You and your sweetie are together now—which means their evaporated time off from work is your evaporated time off from work. But some holidays are better than others when it comes to first impressions.

. . . .

Good Holiday: New Year's

Yes, we know. New Year's Eve is your time to shine. But by "shine," you really mean get drunk and play tonsil hockey with a bunch of randoms. You don't do that anymore, remember? You've gone straight. So swallow that last bit of sexual self-esteem and resign yourself to watching the ball drop with Ryan Seacrest, Fall Out Boy, the cast of *Avenue Q*, and someone else's family, then going to bed at twelve fifteen. You didn't need cold sores again anyway.

Bad Holiday: Christmas

Like Thanksgiving, but worse. On top of the shotgun together-ness, you get the awkward experience of watching a bunch of people you barely know participate in the very personal and often embarrassing process of giving gifts. Stare too long as Dad opens a box full of spandex briefs or Mom tears into a pack of white Hanes panties, and you'll be trying to climb out of that shame hole for years to come.

Good Holiday: Labor/Memorial Day

We pair these two because they're basically the same thing. On Memorial Day, we honor the soldiers who gave their lives in ser-vice to our country. On Labor Day, we honor the guys who stock the shelves at Target late at night. Anyway, both are really about being outdoors with a grill and a moderate amount of beer. This puts family members in a good mood, making them less likely to bring pain to you.

Bad Holiday: St. Patrick's Day

Whereas Labor Day and Memorial Day involve a couple of cans of Coors Light imbibed under a pavilion near the local softball field, St. Patrick's Day usually involves a funnel, green body paint, and being teabagged by a guy named Mike. Under no circumstances do you ever want to be around your significant other's parents on

St. Paddy's. Even seeing *other* people get that wasted is going to damage their impression of you.

Good Holiday: Halloween

Can you think of a better way to show that you can be nice to children—maybe even to the fictitious grandchildren in the potential in-laws' minds—than by smiling and handing out candy? Hell, no. Neither can we.

Bad Holiday: Thanksgiving

Not only will you be introduced to so many family members at once that you'll be calling them all by the wrong names for years to come, but you'll also get to see them at their worst. No holiday yields the tension crop sewn by years of complex family politics more fruitfully than Thanksgiving. Think about it. If you took the same group of people and asked them to get together for a potluck once a year, how long would it be before someone brings a store-bought pie one too many times and all hell breaks loose? Not long. You don't want to be around for that.

SEVEN

THE BREAKUP OPTION: "IT'S NOT ME, IT'S YOU—AND

Your Erectile Dysfunction

B eing in a relationship can sometimes be a thing of awesome. You actually feel good about yourself. You are getting laid on a regular basis. You don't feel like dying inside when you have to pick up the phone because your sweetie's calling. It's incredible—you actually want to do something nice for the other person instead of just feeling on their ass from time to time. But, as we all know, these feelings can sour faster than a carton of 2 percent milk in the sun. When this happens you must do what every person hates to do: fire the person who is giving you free sex.

You have a choice now: learn how to cut your losses and escape without having to ever make reference to your "first marriage," or skip ahead to chapter 8, where you'll begin your journey down the long, treacherous path of commitment. But be warned. Only darkness that way lies. If you're smart, you'll read this chapter, close this book, and go find a drink special somewhere.

. . . .

Quiz

Are you really ready to break it off? Don't do so before you take the following quiz.

Which following statement applies to your current relationship philosophy?

1. Love sucks, then you die. Deal with it.
2. Anything is better than being alone.
3. You shouldn't take your ship out of a safe harbor unless you have another port to call in.

When you think of your significant other . . .

1. A raging anger begins to boil in your gut. You fix yourself a cocktail and drink until the feeling has been numbed to a faint yet constant hum.
2. You smile, realize you're oh-so-lucky to have someone—if only they would learn that toenail clippings do not go into the ashtray. That was your grandmother's goddamn ashtray.
3. You think it would be so much easier if they would just go away. Then you could get out of this gracefully.

The last time you had physical contact was . . .

1. You can't remember but it doesn't matter. The thought of them touching you freezes your insides up like Windows 3.0.
2. Last night. During the deed, you made a list in your head about all the various Swiffer products you needed to buy. Let's see, there was Swiffer WetJet, Swiffer Sweeper, Swiffer Dusters refills . . .
3. You're down to a twice-a-month regime. But, hey, you kissed good-bye this morning on the way to work. That counts, right?

Your kind-eyed elderly neighbors . . .

1. Have started leaving notes on your door to ask you to please limit the shouting to before 10 p.m. and after 8 a.m.
2. Look at you two wistfully. Ask, "So, when's the wedding?" when you take out the garbage. You only smile weakly in turn.
3. Get freaked out when you ask them in a hushed voice if their cute grandchild fresh out of college is still single.

The desire to spawn babies:

1. Babies? Like you need a baby. Jesus Christ, you *live* with one. Then again, maybe that's unfair to babies. At least babies get smarter as time passes. Your significant other

seems to be regressing into some sort of fetal state—and fetuses, as we all know, never do the fucking dishes.

2. Is stronger than your desire to be single again. And, hey, your significant other should make decent breeding stock at the very least.

3. Your biological clock is flashing a giant red "12:00," but you feel absolutely nothing.

YOUR RESULTS

Mostly 1s

Why, hello there, you angry little person. My, you're very, very upset, aren't you? Are you sure all of these rage issues are healthy? Well, they're not. Don't worry about hurting someone by breaking up with them; you're hurting, um, everyone (your family, your friends, your so-called partner, even the guy you buy your coffee from in the morning) by partaking in this hate game. You can find someone who is more compatible, we promise. And, hey, they might even touch you every now and again.

Mostly 2s

You don't want to break up, you just will never know what love is. Kidding! You're in a rut. It happens. The good news is you're not ready to break up. If you want things to improve, you need to take the initiative by being more considerate of the other person in this relationship. "But why should I be nice to them when they're not nice to me?" Well, dear five-year-old friend, let's recall the lessons of your youth. Don't pick your nose in public, and treat others the way you want to be treated. If after genuine, long-term effort to make the relationship more exciting your gestures aren't being reciprocated, it may be time to find a better reciprocator.

Mostly 3s

Six months ago you were in a rut. That rut has now become a ditch—a roadside ditch on the highway of love in which you have upended your Jeep Cherokee 4 x 4 of a relationship. Now is the time to either call AAA (a relationship counselor) or abandon the vehicle.

. . . .

How Can I Tell that I'm Miserable?

The smart dater is always on the lookout for subtle signs that the relationship is going tits-up. These include the hurling of glassware against perfectly good walls, the destruction of (your) cherished childhood mementos, and murder attempts. But some signs are even harder to see than these. Here's what to look out for:

- **Decreased sex activity.** You two used to go at it like rabbits—rabbits that are even hornier than normal rabbits. But these days the sheets aren't getting washed as often as they used to. If sex is being preempted in favor of television, sleeping, or sex with someone else, beware.
- **You only talk when you see each other.** Most couples communicate throughout the day via e-mail, text, even the occasional phone call. This is called keeping tabs. It's

really irritating, but it is a sure sign that the other person cares whether you're lying in a ditch somewhere. If your communication has dwindled to sitting on the couch and asking, "What else is on?" you're in trouble.

- **You fight—a lot.** This should seem like a no-brainer. But for many couples, arguing slowly takes the place of sex as their most frequent hobby without anyone realizing. If you can't follow the simple rule of "Don't yell at each other," you've got some serious thinking to do.

Have Your Exit Strategy in Place

If recent history in the Middle East has taught us one thing, it's the importance of an exit strategy. Usually, the incredibly dull-witted person won't formulate one until they look across the table at lunch one day, notice how the person in front of them is holding a dirty tissue in one hand and a Chipotle burrito in the other, and blurt out, "You're filthier than the New Jersey Turnpike's James Fenimore Cooper Service Area." Thus will begin a series of biweekly, four-hour screaming matches that will last exactly as long as the relationship did. Nixon championed the notion of "peace with honor." He figured that, if he just waited long enough, he could turn the Vietnam War into a success. In a relationship, this is called "making it work."

BE SMART

Have you ever known anyone who made it work? Did your old roommate who called eighteen months ago crying about her boyfriend's Internet affair with a fourteen-year-old girl in Stockholm make it work? No. She became a crazy person.

The smart dater goes into a relationship planning to enjoy as much of it as possible, whether it lasts two months or twenty years, and has a tiny glass box stowed in the back of their mind that says, "Break in case of suckiness." After all, making it work is for chumps who can't embrace the fundamental truth about relationships: They all end. Friends grow apart. Parents move to California and marry twenty-two-year-old lifeguards with no body hair. Lovers become haters. A foolproof breakup line is as important to a lifetime of happiness as a tolerance for gin and a firm abdomen. Take these and hold them close to your heart. Trust us: You'll need them one day.

Foolproof breakup line #1: "I slept with someone else"

This is the hydrogen bomb of breakup lines. You don't actually have to cheat to work this angle, but chances are you already have. Or want to.

Sometimes wars are won through strategic brilliance—and sometimes they're won by firebombing entire cities into rubble. The "I cheated" confession is the most surefire tactic at your disposal, but be prepared for the collateral damage. Not only will you never sleep with that person again, you'll never sleep with anyone in their extended social network, either. To them—and to everyone in your victim's cell phone directory—you are a cheater. You may as well have genital warts. If you live with the person you're trying to dump, prepare to couch surf while they burn your cherished childhood mementos. You'll be granted release from the prison of your relationship, but you'll also forfeit your constitutional rights and be tagged with a permanent record.

Foolproof breakup line #2: "I've found God"

The men and women of your parents' generation were allowed one midlife crisis, and their options were limited. For the guys, there were vintage GTOs and one-night stands with strippers from Tulsa. For the dames, there were housekeepers for hire and classes at the local community college. But we are children of peace, and peace breeds restlessness. The average person born after 1970 will change careers 523 times. It's okay. Your actions don't define who you are. Your iTunes library does.

You're still allowed to have a midlife crisis in the twenty-first century, but you don't have to wait until the middle of your life to do it—and you don't have to do something self-indulgent, morally bankrupt, or pathetically dull. The most admirable way to leave your old life and lover behind is to suffer a crisis of conscience.

Religion has made a cultural comeback in the last fifteen years. If you want to scare away your significant other, choose to walk the path of righteousness.

Are you Jewish? Tell your Episcopalian boyfriend or girlfriend that you're installing a double sink and can only eat kosher from now on. Catholic? Stop having sex and say you want as many children "as the Good Lord will provide." Muslim? Declare a jihad on something. Sure, you'll have to start waking up early on Saturday or Sunday or Friday to drive the point home, but you're saving their feelings—and that's what the Lord would want.

But be careful. Your phony spiritual awakening could prompt an actual religious experience in your prospective ex. If you're not militantly confrontational about your religion, you could wind up sharing a pew for the next forty years with the person you're trying to ditch. Remember: Don't channel the love of Christ. Channel the wrath of an angry God.

Foolproof breakup line #3: "I'm a zombie"

Just say, "Look. This guy, who I thought was homeless and I tried to give change to, totally bit me. Now I'm conflicted. I mean, I guess I'm half human, half 'living dead' (whatever that means). If you don't walk away within the next two minutes, I'm going to be hungry for human flesh and will be forced to infect you with the zombie virus. And that's going to blow for the both of us. And let's face it, I love you too much to have that happen. So run, goddamn you. Run! Run for your life! I'm ch-ch-chan . . . (mmmoooooaaaaannnnn)." Sure, you might have to worry about your face being blown off by a shotgun shortly thereafter, but if the risk is worth it, then go for it.

Foolproof breakup line #4: "I'm a spy"

Start talking about the *21 Jump Street* episode where they had to cut all ties to their past to infiltrate a high school. Say, "I'm sorry, but that is just like what I do. I can't give you any details other than that. But if you want to be my date to the prom, that's cool. Just wait for my call in a few weeks." Normal people will be so creeped out that they will never call you again. Conspiracy theorists will love you and will wait forever or until the time that they go on *Dateline* and tell the story about how they dated a spy. The only evidence will be a few grainy photos and your bad credit checks.

UMM, WHAT?

"Well," you're thinking to yourself right now, "these are all great breakup lines—for liars."

Yes, they are. You're welcome.

"But wait," you say. "I'm not a liar."

Whoziwhatsy?

Okay, we get that some of you might want to tell "the truth" to the person whose life you're about to ruin. It's people like you—you know, people with consciences—who make us want to be better people. We don't try too hard, but we *want* to really be bad. Anyway, for you people, here's how and how not to break up with a human being who, lest we forget, may be legally authorized to purchase a gun in most states.

- **Do not break up with someone at your place of residence.** The reason is simple—the breakee will never leave. They will argue, fight, beg, and plead and probably won't leave unless you use force or bribery.
- **Do break up with someone at a place where an exit is readily handy.** Once home, deadbolt the door and turn off your phone. If you do decide to pick up on the hundredth ring, know that no intelligent, rational conversations about your feelings will take place.
- **Do not break up with someone after they have spent a lot of money on you.** This is just rude. Why leave them with a broken heart after they just bought you a Wii? You can wait a week. Besides, you're more likely to be able to keep the Wii that way.
- **Do break up with someone after you haven't seen each other for a few days.** It's weird to tell someone you just took a weekend road trip with or just received multiple orgasms from that you don't want to ever see them again. Allow for a brief but clear cooling-off period before you detonate the life explosives.
- **Do not break up with someone via text, e-mail, or**

telephone. Technology is a wonderful thing. It made the polio vaccine a reality, as well as TMZ.com. But it can be used for evil as well as good. God did not invent highly advanced communications technology so you could use it to break up with someone. He made it so you can order a Domino's pizza online, then track its progress to your doorstep via the Web site.

- **Do break up with someone in person.** Painful as it is, unless you've been cheated on, abused, or debilitated to the point where you can speak only through one of those Stephen Hawking devices, you owe it to the person you're dumping to do it in the flesh.

Break up with someone in person, right—that's easy for us to say. Well, it is. It's not a very long sentence, and it has no hard-to-pronounce words in it. But unfortunately, there is no foolproof set of talking points to use when dumping someone. No matter what you do, they're likely to get upset. But there is a way to approach the problem in front of you: the way your boss would.

Take a tip from a management book. Corporations have a way to cast off those who are "poisoning the well." It's called "getting fired." And since companies do it so often, they're actually kind of good at it. When you think about it, breaking up with someone is just like firing them. So call early and ask if they can meet you that day (before you chicken out). Make the breakup conversation short and to the point. Be empathetic, but don't let the emotions of the person you're firing affect your own emotions. Remember, the person is being fired for cause. If they get defensive, say, "I'm sorry, but this decision is final." Do not let them linger. But the best part is, you don't have to give them unemployment.

Moving On

After the shock of having to go to bed armed with a paper towel and an anthology of literary erotica instead of a real, live human being wears off, you'll be back to your old cynical self. In a few months, you'll fall back to your weekend routine of rolling over at 2 p.m., lighting a Camel, and watching *Dickie Roberts: Former Child Star* on cable. Your other single friends will welcome you back with open arms. You can now distribute your dirty underwear at random on your floor. You don't have to shower or shave. You can make out with your choice of drunks at the bar with no feelings of remorse the day after. You can update your online dating profile for shits and giggles. Enjoy this time.

. . . .

HE SAYS/SHE SAYS

Should you take the high road when dumped?

He Says: Yes!

When the person you're dating ends the relationship, it's important to remember that they're not just dumping you—they're dumping a part of themselves. It's natural to spend days sitting naked, staring at your reflection on the TV screen, thinking, "No one will ever love this again. As I grow older, fatter, and wrinklier, my prospects of finding someone will only decrease. Why doesn't Carvel have a delivery service?" You've earned these feelings. Enjoy.

What you haven't earned is the right to blame the other person for your misery. As much pain as you're going through, know that they are experiencing the same pain. Sure, they express it differently. While you stand in the kitchen, wondering what it would feel like to carve their name into the sole of your foot, your ex is at '80s dance night, making out with every college senior within ass-grabbing distance. That does not make their hurt less real.

You have lost the battle for love, but you must not lose the battle for your soul. When you head to White Castle alone in your pajamas at 1 a.m. and find your ex there, accompanied by a crew of people more attractive than Rihanna's backup dancers, do not pelt the ex with Chicken Rings. Instead, walk over and extend the Chicken Ring of friendship. You'll feel better about yourself tomorrow.

She Says: Low Road

You know what's awesome about being a girl (besides having boobs)? The fact that we are excellent at being catty. We spend day in and day out trying to suppress this God-given talent, but now, in the fit of a breakup, is the perfect time to let it all out, ladies. Let the nastiness fly. Although you will be judged by the people behind you for cursing at the drive-through attendant for taking too long, everyone understands that you have free rein to take it to the man who scorned you. Get it out. Stand under his bedroom window and scream and plead for a second chance. Leave his things on his doorstep and set them on fire. Tell his friends about how he liked to call you "Mommy." Change all of his Internet pass codes. Hire a clown to follow him around. You are one crazy psycho bitch! You go, girl!

The good thing about being cathartically vengeful is that it gets tiresome. After week three of screaming into his voice mail, you'll get tired. You just need to exorcise the hurt of being dumped. Once that clears through the pure force of your abject bitchiness, you can go back to being antagonistic to your Chinese deliveryman for not including your egg roll order *again*.

. . . .

TIMELINE OF DESPAIR

However, if you're the one who was broken up with, we now present to you your timeline of despair. No matter how long the relationship or how involved you were, you will feel some level of this anguish. But, everyone says, you can, at a certain point, get on with your life. The length of grief over being dumped is relative to the length of a relationship. For, say, a six-monther, there is a simple timeline of stages that every person who has even been broken up with goes through. Here it is. Embrace your future.

Days one through three
Tears. Lots and lots of tears. You will not be able to get out of bed. You will call your ex at numerous random times throughout the day and night, not saying anything but holding the phone up to some Smiths song that is playing from your clock radio as you sob in the background.

Days four through seven
Lack of appetite will be replaced with appetite. Consumption of foodstuffs will be used to try to fill the void in your soul. Your new best friends are Ho Hos, marshmallow pies, milk shakes,

Chinese food, and Fritos. TBS will be the station of choice on the TV set. Your ex has changed phone numbers by this point, but you can still read their blog. Read and reread until you convince yourself their constant references to a particular coworker means they were having an affair the entire time. Cry more.

Days eight through eleven

The phone calls to people who aren't your ex begin. You will call your mom and blame her for fucking you up so bad that no one will ever love you. Call your friends and ask them if you have bad breath. Call your therapist at home and beg for an appointment. Alternate watching TBS with ESPN specials on which Peyton Manning plays touch football with a terminally ill kid. Cry more.

Day twelve

You will have to try to actually do some work. Go out with the mailroom guys or the middle-aged front desk receptionist for happy hour. Get wasted. Ask them if they find you attractive. Force them to drive you home and desperately try to suck face with them. Remember nothing.

Days thirteen through twenty

You will be drunk every night and hungover every morning. The good thing is, you will be too dehydrated to cry. At night, watch Netflix romantic comedies you requested back when someone still loved you. The insipidness of Sarah Jessica Parker and/or Sandra Bullock makes you hate love.

Days twenty through thirty

Anger will reign. Embrace it. Being angry means you can throw out their personal belongings instead of clutching them to your chest as you try to fall asleep. Being angry means you can "unfriend" them from MySpace instead of constantly scoping their profile to see if they are "in a relationship" or not. Being angry will cause you to bad-mouth their lack of sexual prowess to anyone who will listen instead of cooing about what a sensitive lover they were. Think about joining Bikram yoga and getting a cat.

Days thirty-one and on and on and on

The anger that was once all-encompassing will now be just a tiny little ball that you will keep forever in your damaged heart. This isn't so bad. You are now ready to move on to your next relationship and/or start a career in stand-up. Have fun!

AND JUST WHEN YOU THINK IT'S OVER . . .

Congratulations! Your hairline may be receding or your breasts may hang a half inch lower than they did a few years ago, but you won't let aging force you to act your age. You've kept the demon of adulthood at bay. You've destroyed a relationship with real potential before it could mature. It's time for you to put on clean underwear—or none at all—and get to an '80s night (preferably one near a college campus).

But wait. You see that pile of clothes in the corner? The one you were this close to urinating on three nights ago? It's still early. You have time to drop that stuff off at their place before you go out. It's the mature thing to do.

Make sure you bring a condom.

You've finally buried the hurt feelings and sense of suffocation under strata of booze, pills, and chicken wings. You've given your ex time to do the same. Now their bed calls to you like the voice of Sauron in a hobbit's ear. The pit stains in their T-shirts and the way they talked to their mother on the phone in that Elmo-from-*Sesame Street* voice have all faded in your brain to a soft white noise of past discontent. The only vivid memory you can dig up right now is the second time you had sex . . . on the floor . . . of the library. What happens next is the second reason you won't forget this night anytime soon. You will lie flat on your back, having drained every ounce of water through your sweat glands, and stare blankly at the ceiling. Then your ex will reach over and touch you—and not in a "So, you wanna go again?" way. No, your ex will touch you on the arm. And you will freak the fuck out.

No sex brings the pain quite like return-to-the-well sex. You will reach for your pants, and your ex will emit a high-frequency sonic screech that will wake up every dog and autistic middle schooler within a two-mile radius. Then the crying starts—and the throwing of things. Your ex will wear the psychological scars from this evening for the rest of their life. You will wear a splint or an eye patch. Healing from a broken relationship takes time, and you just picked the scab off. As a reward, you'll get the gift of running out the front door as shards of the bedside lamp embed themselves in the soles of your feet. Don't say we didn't warn you.

MY COLD FEET ARE GIVING ME COLD FEET

But what if you've gotten this far and you think you have a good thing going? You're just feeling uncertain, because for a twenty-first century American making the decision between the value meals #3 and #4 is tough, never mind making a life decision. Simply put, everyone wants the Baconator, but is another choice a bit better for you in the long run? As Flannery O'Connor once wisely put it, "A good man is hard to find," and Ron Jeremy, in between sex scenes, put it succinctly: "Sex is simple—love is painful." It's much easier to be single, that's for sure. But finding someone you want to be with is exhausting. Get this through your head: You'll never, ever, ever find someone who is perfect. Everyone settled—do you think that Bill Clinton really wanted to be attached to Hillary for the rest of his life? Jesus, no. But there is a point where you need to say to yourself, "Fuck it. I really, really like this person. Let's see where this goes." If your gut tells you to keep trying, then by all means, keep trying. And pray there won't be a Monica Lewinsky (or a Kenneth Starr) in your future.

Finishing Off

Alfred, Lord Tennyson once said, "'Tis better to have loved and lost than never to have loved at all." To that person, we say, "You're an idiot." When all is said and done, we don't remember the love—we only remember the agony of having our hearts ripped out of our chests. The breakup is something no one wants to go through, but we must, so that we may know what it's like to look terror in the face. Sure, breaking up with someone or having them break up with you brings terrible psychological damage, but think about a life without breakups: Therapists wouldn't have jobs. Children of divorce would be well-adjusted instead of working in HR. Girls wouldn't be so eager to take their tops off, and guys wouldn't obey their every command just because they did. And perhaps most importantly, you wouldn't have any "crazy-psycho ex" stories to entertain your bar buddies with.

But for those who aren't ready to hit the reset button on love, read on, brave reader. Read on.

EIGHT

THE DEATH OF ROMANCE (OR HOW I LEARNED TO STOP WORRYING AND

Love Paying Half As Much Rent

Back a long, long, long time ago, a couple living together without first being married was an anomaly of the most sluttastic proportions. This just didn't happen. It was improper, and you would be persecuted by friends, family, and townsfolk in a way that would make the witches of colonial Salem say, "Oh, now, that's just wrong." Now, thankfully, people have a little more common sense (they didn't even *know* about hybrid cars back then, for Chrissake). By evolving, we've come to realize that not only is moving in together not an act of Satan's doing, but it also saves thousands of dollars on divorce lawyers once you have the startling revelation that the beautiful person you thought you wanted to spend your life with has a habit of blowing their nose into their socks in the middle of the night.

Besides making sure that you aren't legally bound to a roommate you come to loathe, moving in together before marriage saves you an assload in rent. Love schmove. The chance to spend less money on the cable bill and more on the pay-per-view movies that don't come with basic cable is the number one reason couples take this step. As anyone who's been cruelly separated from their mother's teat knows, rent is really expensive nowadays—especially since you lost your job because of that little plagiarism scandal or blew through your trust fund on trips to Burning Man and a pot habit that Ricky Williams would admire.

Sometimes, you just really, really like someone and want to be with them at all times. So it makes perfect sense to the both of you to move in together. If this is the case, kudos to you. But please, take some advice from two people who have done it: take a few days and really, really think about it. Love fades but the dirty socks on the floor—which have never made it into the hamper (ever!)—don't. Those socks will never move, but your love will change. As we've said, moving in is a very serious step, one that gets real life (aka personal habits) and love into a huge, bloody smackdown. Most of the best friends in the world become roommates and within six months never speak again. But if you are two people who are kind, gentle, and loving enough to look past all of these things, then by all means, go for it. Just be sure to invite us to the wedding.

Speaking of weddings, love and money aren't the only factors to consider when making major life decisions. If they were, we'd all be loading up on rifles and buying huge tracts of land in Costa Rica for our love nests (it's so cheap there!). So why else do couples take this gargantuan step—one that is arguably more momentous than any other in a relationship? Because in the end, by moving in together you are facilitating two things: (1) either expediting a breakup (the awfulness of which will be compounded by having to move out), or (2) speeding along an engagement, because you will have nothing to talk about other than how your mother won't speak to you now that she's convinced your current living situation has damned you to hell (most moms are still puritans at heart).

Unfortunately, many couples think of neither of these things before the big move. They are blinded by the aforementioned savings in rent and the fact they will live with someone a little less annoying than their current roommate—with an added bonus of being granted free rein to their special parts. This sounds like free candy to a couple—free candy that tastes like sex and money.

Fools!

How It Happens

Basically, treat moving in together as though you were getting engaged (but without the expense of buying a ring and having a wedding). Too soon into the relationship, and everyone will be shaking their heads ("It's just too soon!"). Too far along, then everyone will know it won't happen. Still confused? Give the relationship a year of serious, exclusive dating, then have the talk. Also keep in mind that if you're young, you have a lot of time to move in together. If you're old, then no.

It's daunting to figure out how eliminating all personal space is a good idea. (Well, when you put it like that it is, anyway.) It's actually quite simple: You are part of a couple now. You no longer make late-night booty calls. Your toothbrush has had a firm spot in your sweetie's bathroom for quite a while. You have each other's keys. You are, to quote every single person who has ever moved in together, "spending every night together anyway." So the conversation eventually moves to moving in together. This is normal. Stop freaking out.

Of course, there is also the flip to this: the instances of Relationships on Speed. This is when you fall madly in lust with someone and somehow they do the same right back atcha. You, in turn, blitzkrieg them with "I have never felt this way, and I want to take our relationship to the next level." They, being just as crazy and needy as you, will agree and show up the next morning with a duffel bag full of their clothing. This Relationship on Speed move-in usually doesn't work. Neither you nor your partner is worn-down enough from the everyday drudgery of a long-term relationship to stop thinking about what else is out there. With the blitzkrieg, you move too quickly. You never forget how to stop thinking like a single person. It's all too much, too soon. You become overloaded by the sudden invasion of new colors, new smells, constant sex.

Sadly, the blitzkrieg will just break the other person, not tame them into the manageable little domestic partner you need them to be. No, you need to wear the other person down slowly, so they are trained and can use the bathroom properly before you start sharing one.

. . . .

Quiz

Are you ready to share a living space with someone you care for? Take this quiz to find out.

Wondering if your prospective roomie is emotionally ready, you do some inspecting.

1. You find they have already changed their address, bought a Cuisinart mixer, and purchased moving supplies.
2. Whenever you bring up the subject, they shrug their shoulders, slam a Miller High Life, and try to take off your pants.
3. You open their closet door. A family of meerkats peers up at you. You think of asking your boyfriend/girlfriend what this is all about, but instead you disappear out the fire escape, never to return.

Your boyfriend/girlfriend's current roommate . . .

1. Dreads the idea of having to live with anyone else. Your sweetie, it turns out, thinks the best way to unwind after a long day at work is to roll up the ol' sleeves and have a go at a sink full of dirty dishes.
2. Seems concerned only with the idea that you may choose to move into this apartment and give him or her the boot. Most of your conversations consist of them telling you about how awful the landlord is, how they think they saw a rat one time, and how the upstairs neighbors like to have really loud sex that involves a lot of screaming of the words "hurt me" and "bowling ball."
3. Spends way too much time telling you what a rewarding experience living together will be. You've made an excellent life decision—really, you have. Would you mind if

they put up an ad on Craigslist looking for a new room-mate? No reason to wait when you're talking about true love, after all.

Your sweetie's record collection . . .

1. Consists of MP3s. Why take up all that space when it's so much easier to have those songs on the computer?
2. Is limited to some hand-me-down LPs from their parents. Yeah, that stuff's heavy, but one of these days you're going to be dying to hear "Up on Cripple Creek," and you really don't want to pay ninety-nine cents for it on iTunes.
3. Was written up in *CMJ* magazine. It turns out that sweetie was the music director at the college radio station back in the day, and that bookcase full of free-jazz LPs you just called junk is, in fact, the most extensive to be found outside of Chicago. If you think you're putting even one of those out in a stoop sale, you'd best think again.

You consider having personal space . . .

1. Fine, although sometimes you get scared of the occasional brutal home invasion that your nightly news is so keen on reporting.
2. Important. You need two hours a day of alone time. If not, you're one cranky bitch.

3. A necessity to your meditation practices. You can't under-state the significance of your mindfulness, concentration, tranquility, and insight. If you don't get fourteen hours in a week, you feel as though you have failed your master, Sunim Ho, who has the corner shop above the neigh-borhood pet store. He says you have only twenty-three more years (give or take a few months) until you achieve enlightenment. Not bad for a whitey!

Your current roommate . . .

1. You don't have one. You figured that at the age of twenty-seven, it was time to stop living like a frat boy and be the master of your own domain. Besides, last time you had a roommate, they made fun of the fact that you lined your drawers with scented paper. And really, doesn't everyone know that unlined drawers are a sign of being uncivilized?
2. Is a buddy from college who you haven't really been able to shake.
3. Is a conspiracy theorist and hasn't left your place since 2003. Even though you have no idea what they download all the day long, at least they keep to themselves.

YOUR RESULTS

Mostly 1s

Moving in together is a major step, but you're more pre-pared for it than a Chinese exchange student is for the math portion of the SATs. Go ahead and house hunt.

Mostly 2s

It's going to be a tough, unorganized move, but keep reminding yourself how much you're in love with this person. Failing that, develop a hobby. We suggest downers.

Mostly 3s

You know what? Maybe a lifetime of solitude is good for the soul. Think of all the work you'll get done with no one else around. If it was good enough for Thoreau, it's good enough for you.

How to Start

There are three ways to move in together: (1) you move in with them, (2) they move in with you, (3) you find your own place together. Of course, we've heard of situations where couples move in with one of their parents. And, wow, we don't even know what to say to that except for "Don't."

Picking one of these options sounds easy, right? Just go with the place that is largest, cheapest, and closest to work. Of course, not everyone's partner will have an amazing, huge, city apartment with tons of closet space that you can just waltz into without a fuss. All move-ins require patience, fortitude, and a good deal of fussitude. Weigh the pros and cons of all your options in a fair and balanced manner; then whine, scream, and cry until the other person agrees to move into your place. Let's show you why.

THE HOBBLING: YOU DECIDE TO MOVE INTO THEIR SPACE

Even though Sandra Oh kept her apartment after she moved in with the homophobe on *Grey's Anatomy*, it's important to understand that we can't all be sexy but odd-looking Asian TV doctors with loads of cash. By moving into their space, you will have to give up your own. But there's a very real chance this cohabitation might not work. Then you'll be just as good as those homeless people you scowl at on your way to work. You will have to mend a broken heart and couch surf at the same time, a combination that would put even Rachael Ray into a dark, Sylvia Plathesque depression.

You will also have to move, and as our Native American friends know, moving sucks. To lessen the pain, insist that your sweetie split the price of moving with you. Yes, you could come off as a cheapskate, but fair is fair. By moving into someone else's place, not only are you saving them the trouble of moving their stuff, you're also saving them the cost. It's crazy important to establish early in the game that you won't be taken advantage of financially. We're not saying that person who you are so totally in love with after four long months of booty calls and Netflix is out to get you. But financial stress will make the most considerate of lovers do shitty things without even realizing it.

By the way, we're not talking about splitting one of those $29-a-day U-Hauls. You're hiring movers. Because no matter how much you ply your friends with beer, they will never forgive you for having to hump your shit up three flights of stairs for the fourth time in five years. Hell, most of them stopped answering your calls after last time. (You think that TV was dropped by accident?) Get a mover. Your sweetie will be happy that the thugs you invited into the place aren't your exes.

Once the date is set for the big move, the apartment will be hypothetically yours and should have space for your things. If you leave it to your new roomie to create this space, you'll arrive on moving day to find you have to cram a lifetime's worth of possessions into two drawers and one kitchen cabinet shelf. Take it upon yourself to spend a weekend ahead of the move at "your" new place reorganizing the other person's life for them. A pain in the ass? Yes, but forty-three pairs of shoes don't just store themselves.

EXCUSES, EXCUSES

By now, we hope you realize that moving in together means you can no longer stay out until 4 a.m. with randoms at the bar. Sex on the sly will be impossible. You will have no more alone time again ever in your entire life. If you're having second thoughts or, you know, complete freak-outs, there's still time, friend. If you've come to the realization that there is no way in hell you can do this, good for you. Better to pack it in now. After all, if you really would rather make out with strangers at a bar than sit at home watching HBO while the person next to you nods off at 11 p.m., you shouldn't be doing this. Here are some tried and tested excellent excuses to throw around to make sure you keep your independent spirit—as well as your collection of vintage Pabst Blue Ribbon canisters—intact.

"I've talked with my landlord and my lease is impossible to break until [made-up date]."
Rationale: Most people don't speak renter-ese. We just send our rent check every month and hope for the best. This will be a digestible excuse to take; you have time to think of another way to get out of this until the date your lease supposedly ends.

"My parents don't believe in cohabitation before marriage."

Rationale: No one wants to be seen as a person with loose morals, even if loose morals are what constitute your entire being. Of course, when you are ready, your parents' opinion won't matter one hot damn. But this excuse will buy you an endless amount of time. Should you change your mind and decide to go through with the move, just say that you finally talked to your parents and put your foot down. "I told them it's my life and my decision, not theirs." You'll come out of this smelling better than ever. Nothing is more attractive than the notion of living with someone whose parents will never come for a visit.

"I can't sleep at night, I'm so nervous. I don't think I'm ready."

Rationale: No one wants to move in with a basket case—that's what the other person's past six roommates were, and he or she probably doesn't want a seventh. The other person should respect your complete anxiety about this step. If not, well, you're probably going to break up anyway.

MOVING CHECKLIST

Do: Alert proper people of your new address. The post office, bank accounts, credit cards, employer, IRS, and your dying great-uncle who has no kids of his own and a helluva lot of IBM stock he bought in 1952.

Don't: Let these people know if you are on the lam.

Do: Pack up the small stuff and move it gradually. Start dropping boxes over at the other person's place a month in advance, starting with your "private" things first. If they freak out about your Incredible Hulk resin statue collection or *Sex and the City* box set, you still have time to rethink.

Don't: Go home tanked, throw all of your shit into boxes, cram them into your Subaru, and show up at 4:30 in the a.m., proclaiming, "Honey, I'm home!" This is not as cute and romantic as you think.

Do: Let your current landlord know. (We can't believe we even had to remind you of that.)

Don't: Call your new landlord on moving day and say, "I'm staring at a wall that looks like it hasn't been painted since Howard Dean looked like presidential material. If I were you, I'd hop in the landlordmobile with a bucket and brush and get your ass over here, because there's a new sheriff in town, motherfucker."

· ·

Protect Yourself

You don't have to worry about getting herpes from a stranger, but you still have to protect yourself. Not to get all Suze Orman up in your shit, but before you move in, it is wise to start an ING or other Internet savings account that takes a hundred bucks a month out of your checking. That way, after a year or so, if things go sour, you have some money safely tucked away to hire those thug movers again and some cash to put toward a security deposit on your own bachelor pad of shame. If you're lucky, you might have enough left over to buy a decent bottle of Scotch or a couple of therapy sessions. Your sweetie may be willing to help financially with the move-in, but moving out is on your head. If, praise Jesus, things work out, you two love-birds now have the cash you need to replace that couch or buy a blender—you lame-os, you.

. . . .

Safe at home: Turning your place into "ours"

Good work. Thanks to your persuasive rhetorical skills (or sexual bribery), your apartment will be turned into a happy home for two. Watching a moving truck full of someone else's stuff pull up to your building might feel like spotting an army of Huns on the horizon, but in this case it's better to be the invadee than the invader. Yes, the city gates will be breached, but you'll have time to prepare for the foreign hordes and hide the valuables.

The first order of business is clearing half the apartment's storage space for your new roomie. But wait, didn't we tell you that it's best for the person moving to do that? Yes—if *you're* the person moving. The person who organizes the apartment holds the upper hand in deciding what stays and what goes. We want you to be that person. Why? Because you're the one who bought this book. You're like family to us. Your sweetie is just some in-law we barely tolerate. For instance, if you have a closet with two shelves, clear off the top one. The other person can't complain, because you've provided them with equal space (which was more than they were expecting). But you're not the one who will need a ladder to reach your board games. And that carton of dashikis you haven't worn since sophomore year of college? Stash it under the back of the bed before the move, and you can put off that trip to Goodwill for at least another year or two. Yes, you will have to get rid of stuff—lots of stuff. But by taking responsibility for making your apartment a welcoming place to move into, you can avoid coming home to find half your record collection on the floor next to a note that says, "When was the last time you listened to these?" Plus, your significant other will see your efforts as an attempt to make things easier on them in this traumatic time.

CHECKLIST

Do: Hide love letters and all other traces of past relationships far, far away. Your relationship may be built on a foundation of trust, but the ground underneath is prone to occasional mudslides of snoopiness. This is an argument you can avoid; you really shouldn't be asked to throw these mementos away because how else, when you are old and infirm (about two years from now), will you be able to remember those days when you got plenty of tail?

Don't: Keep referring your place as "my apartment." This is rude. That will make any man's testicles ascend and women feel like indentured sex slaves. You can continue to think those thoughts, but remember the advice of your father: "For God's sake, just shut up. Just shut up before I make you shut up."

Do: Work out a bill-paying plan. If your utilities are hooked up online to your bank account, sit down together with a calendar, look at your pay schedules and the bills' due dates, and set days for the other person to write you checks for their share. Remember, you're doing this so you both can save money—emphasis on "both."

Don't: Open a joint checking account. Moving in together is a first step toward a long-term commitment. Joint checking may be in your future, but for now you need to focus on emotional compatibility and learning to share a space.

Do: Get a maid. With the money you are saving, you should be able to pay someone who makes slightly less than you to come in and pick up socks and period underwear. Love is many things, but it is not a toilet that smells like ass.

Don't: Ever tell the other person to do the dishes. Doing dishes sucks, but being unloved sucks more. Just do the dishes yourself, you stupid baby.

There's no "my place" in "team": Finding an apartment together

Oddly, the easiest way to move in together may also be the most expensive and time-consuming. If you can't move into each other's places, you've moved together to a new town, or both of your apartments have more bad history than the Amityville Horror, it might be time to visit your old friend Craigslist—or, if you are more upwardly mobile, a real-life real estate agent. This will take way more elbow grease than the usual move, as you will spend your days looking at apartments, talking about prices, discussing whether you want the house with the washing machine or the condo with the garden porch, and plotting ingenious ways to break your leases. However, starting off on equal footing can be worth the extra work.

Instead of forcing you to look at a lived-in space and think, "What will I have to give up?" a new place gives you the opportunity to say, "What can *we* do with this?" Living together is going to be about learning to make decisions together. It's easier to decide what to put on a wall when you don't have to first decide whether to take down what's already on it.

Also, we know you're in this to save some dough, but consider getting a two bedroom. No, you don't have to sleep in separate beds like some old couple who stayed together for the kids and can't stand the smell of each other anymore. But a second room can be turned into a study or sex gym and provides you a lot more storage space—essential when two become one. It gives you someplace to go besides the public house when you have a fight. "But we never fight," you say. Well, that's because until now you've been living in a fairy-tale world of sleepovers and separate addresses. Welcome to the world of shattered individuality. We've been waiting for you.

Once you've decided how much space you want, you need to pick a maximum dollar amount you're willing to spend on rent. If life has been kind, you and your mate have annual salaries within $5,000 of each other. But as the slow melting of Nicolas Cage's face shows us, life is seldom kind. Chances are one of you makes a lot more money than the other. It would make sense that one of you would contribute more toward the rent than the other. Don't do it. No matter how much you both say you're cool with this notion, you're not. Whoever ends up paying more will feel deep down that they're being taken. Whoever is paying less will feel deep down that the other person feels deep down that they are being taken. These tiny pearls of resentment will bury themselves deep in your chests, where they'll slowly grow until one day one of them is coughed up in the form of an angry tirade.

If you're the cash cow in the relationship, you need to resign yourself to downgrading your neighborhood. No, you won't be as close to the Whole Foods or that specialty cheese shop where the owner's wife knows to set aside a half pound of Urgelia every other week for you. But your new nabe will have a bodega called Best Guy on Block and a garage where you can buy used tires. It will also have no resentment.

If you're the one who failed at life and can't find a job with health insurance, much less a decent salary, get yourself on as tight a budget as possible so your sweetie doesn't have to feel like they're regressing to be with you. Yes, no matter what you do, your new place won't be as nice as their swank condo in the doorman building uptown. But it doesn't have to be down the street from a storefront window with a hand-painted sign that says "Crack Cocaine Rehabilitation Center." Drinking a few fewer beers on the weekend will do wonders for your wallet, your waistline, and your relationship.

. . . .

Real Estate:
An Investment in Disaster

Consider the difficulties of moving into a new rental together. Now compound those headaches by a thousand. That's what buying a place will be like. Investing in an apartment or house together while not being legally wed shouldn't even be considered unless you are planning on getting hitched, like, tomorrow. Breaking up is bad. Breaking up while living together is even worse. And a breakup in which you will probably have to take legal action to recoup your fair share of a giant investment is the holocaust of splits. Wait for that undertaking until you are married, so if you get divorced you can have pricey lawyers figure all that shit out for you.

Livin' la vida Cuisinart

Assuming you decided not to opt out at the last minute (or your partner saw through those bullshit lines we just gave you—who did you think you were fooling with that stuff?), the transition doesn't end after the moving van pulls away and the boxes are unpacked. You are now being domesticated. Don't believe it? We laugh inwardly at you. See if any of these telling signs sound familiar.

- You have stopped referring to your friends as "being in the on-deck circle."
- Morning breath ceases to disgust you.
- You find the period underwear—and you just sort of shrug at it, like it's an unruly child that can't be given away.
- You start checking your mailbox for the Crate and Barrel catalog.
- Instead of happy hour, you begin to look forward to TBS marathons of *Everybody Loves Raymond*.
- You invite other couples over for Par-cheese-y, your aptly named board games-and-cheese night.
- Your leg hair, which last rose above surface level during your brief hippy period freshman year, now grows at a kudzulike rate.
- An ex-fuck buddy you once referred to as Miracle Mouth

calls. You say you're sorry, you just don't remember her, and hang up the phone.

- You pick up the phone to make a hair appointment, then think, "Why bother?" and walk down the street to Supercuts.
- Checking the mail sounds really, really exciting right now.
- An ex-fuck buddy you once referred to as the Tommy the Tongue calls. You throw the phone into the fish tank.
- Whichever online networking site you're currently wasting time with at work now states in proud HTML that you are "in a relationship."

· ·

HE SAYS/SHE SAYS

Will moving in together be good for your sex life?

He Says: Yes! Many non-awesome things (sharing a bathroom, sharing a television) come with living together. But there is one very awesome thing that makes up for it: sex all the hot damn time.

Cohabitation means no more hopping on a crosstown bus when the urge strikes. Simply roll over, roll the other person over, and begin coitus. It's that simple.

Easy access isn't the only aspect of life together that will spur your sex life. You will also see a lot more of each other naked. Never mind that *Seinfeld* episode where Jerry's improbably hot girlfriend is naked all the time and he hates it.

There is no such thing as bad naked. Naked is always good, because naked means that sex can happen at any moment—in the shower, while dinner is cooking, while dinner is being eaten, etc.

Best of all, you will lie down next to your partner every night and wake up next to them every day. This guarantees you at least two daily opportunities for sex. With odds like that, how can you lose? Now, if you can only convince your mate to sleep naked. Before you know it, you'll be having more sex than R. Kelly at a junior high girls' basketball tournament.

She Says: No! Ah, you've fallen for the Great Shared Bedroom hoax: you think that because you *can* have sex whenever you want it, you will. But, honey, just because you got that coupon for a free pack of Extra in *Parade* magazine last weekend doesn't mean you are going to claim it. This is what happens: You're both on the couch, and the thought of doing it passes through your head. But you're tired, you ate too much at dinner, and a new episode of *Heroes* is on. Wouldn't it be much easier to wait until tomorrow morning when you are both fresh and happy? Then tomorrow morning comes, and one of you wants to sleep in. Why the rush? You can do it later; after all, you now live together.

The problem is the urgency is no longer there. Back when your parents were still talking to you and you lived in separate abodes, the need to do it was there because you never knew when opportunity would next be available. Your body needed you to stock up. Your loins, nervous that the well would suddenly dry up, would say to your brain, "Must sex now!" Now that you live together, it seems silly to press the matter (or press up against your new roommate), because you just figure there will be a better time later down the line. But soon domesticity will set in, and having sex will become just another chore you do around the house (and never in the back of a cab).

In Conclusion

The late, great Marvin Gaye once sang, "It takes two, baby, to make a dream come true, just takes two." Marvin Gaye was also gunned down by his own father in 1984, meaning that it also "takes two" to drive someone to destruction. But don't worry. We're sure moving in together is the right next step for you—even if it isn't. Because there comes a time in everyone's relationship when they have to oh-so-romantically "shit or get off the pot." And cohabitation is the burrito-and-Scotch combo to get the job done.

NINE

GOING TO

the Chapel . . .

e date for one reason: so that we don't have to do it anymore. We want to stop meeting near strangers for activities that aren't fun. We want to stop feeling lonely and desperate. We want to stop walking into our house to be greeted only by small, dependent animals. We want to settle into the life of routine and endless servitude called marriage. But why is marriage so much more of a popular option than just living with someone for the rest of your life, you wonder? We have no idea, but it usually has something to do with the fact that your friends are doing it and it's what your parents want.

Now that you are in a serious relationship, your weekends are planned days in advance.

You're allowing hair to grow where it has not grown in years. When your friends catch you flirting with a random at a bar, they pull you aside, shake you by the shoulder, and whisper, "But you're with someone." You shrug drunkenly and say, "Yeah, but I'm not married."

Well, maybe it's time you did something about that.

Being married is exactly like your current state of being but with better appliances. You're already shacked up. You already ask each other for permission to do anything that doesn't involve spending five hours of watching HBO On Demand. So why not publicly acknowledge the relationship that, according to God and common law, you are already living *and* receive four dozen wineglasses?

You have your reasons—and they are bullshit. Let's call them out, shall we?

"I CAN WALK AWAY AT ANY TIME"

This is the same lie that heroin addicts and *Passions* viewers tell themselves every day. You continue to justify your current situation by saying to yourself late at night, when the sleep won't come and your partner is snoring directly into your ear canal, "The day this gets out of control is the day when I put on my walking shoes."

Except your joint lease doesn't run out for another eight months. You both put money into that couch. You bought and named that cat together. The prospect of packing your things into boxes while dodging books being thrown at you by your jilted lover seems like a hell of a lot of work. And worst of all, if you walk, you are the one who is going to have to field the endless string of questions from your mother as to why you decided to throw away a perfectly good relationship. She's not getting any younger, you know, and it's not like your brother, the night manager at Pizza Hut, is going to be making grandbabies (legitimate ones, anyway) anytime soon.

"I DON'T BELIEVE IN MARRIAGE"

People don't believe in Santa Claus or Jesus. Not believing in marriage is like not believing in rednecks. They're everywhere, they've been around forever, and just because you've never seen one that works doesn't mean they don't exist.

Yes, marriage is a little quaint and more than a little silly. But there are reasons people do it—practical reasons. Say your loved one is in a horrific accident. How will you claim their Social Security benefits later in life if the two of you aren't married? Second homes in Costa Rica don't just buy themselves, you know. And look at your friends. They too once spent many a late hour with you at the bar decrying the institution of marriage, but now it seems like everyone in your social circle somehow got hitched along the way. Isn't it easier to join their debates at parties on how to clean an engagement ring, the logistics of filing a joint tax return, how to introduce getting head back into your relationship, and the current fads of IVF treatments rather than rail against these boring, exclusive conversations? Speaking of your friends, have you noticed that for some strange reason, you are starting to feel a bit guilty that you haven't returned the favor of being invited to their nuptials and now feel the uncontrollable urge to host them for a weekend of vows, bland hors d'oeuvres, and open bar at your hometown country club? Yeah, it's weird, isn't it? Sure, you don't believe in marriage, but you've slowly come around to the idea of having a wedding—and somehow have fooled yourself into thinking one doesn't beget the other.

"WHAT IF I'M NOT A GOOD WIFE OR HUSBAND?"

It's totally natural to feel intimidated by the roles of husband and wife. Most of us aren't Huxtables, after all (because most of us are not affluent black people with forty-seven children). There have always been certain expectations that come with marriage. But thanks to the bizarre state of American middle-class life, they're all pretty much gone now. Husbands, you don't have to be the provider. No one expects you to afford a three-bedroom in the burbs and dual hybrid SUVs on your salary alone. And, wives, so what if you don't know how to do laundry or change a diaper? That's why you work eleven hours a day—so you can pay someone to clean your house and raise your child for you.

Of course you don't know how to be a good husband or wife. No one knows how. But just as you somehow devised ways to pass yourself off as a functioning adult, so too will you learn to play your spousal role with the acting ability of Ben Kingsley—or at the very least a mediocre Claire Danes. As long as you don't engage in behavior that would make Dr. Phil speechless (wouldn't that be something?) or send your future spawn forever into therapy (we're talking the big no-no's like hitting, cheating, drinking, or any combination of the three). Just be boring and complacent, and give it up every now and again. You'll be in the running for Spouse of the Year for all eternity.

"THIS ISN'T THE ONE"

If you are holding out because you've convinced yourself that, although you've fallen in love with this imperfect person, he or she "just isn't the one," we say to that, "Well, who cares?"

Yes, since you were a young adolescent you've had this ideal life partner living in your head. The perfect yin to your yang with whom you will fight the evils of life and conquer whatever obstacles come your way, all the while becoming rich and staying more beautiful/thin than you ever imagined. And your current beau, well, isn't this person.

Compared to the other excuses, this is quite valid. But think: Have you ever met anyone that you thought could be the one? Even kind of one-ish? Probably not—which is why you're in your current situation. It's not easy finding someone who looks past your own imperfections and has none of their own. Along the way you will have to partake in a little activity we like to call "settling." Think of it this way: you will either settle for a middle-of-the-road life of PTA meetings, hospital visits, weddings, funerals, graduations, and death with someone that marriage brings you, or you will do this all alone. It's your pick.

Onward and upward

Now that we've decided that yes, marriage seems like an okay thing, here's how you do it. Ladies, we're talking to you. Gentlemen, all you have to do is ask—not the easiest thing in the world, but unless you're sterile, it's not like you have much convincing to do. Girls, you have the tough job: tricking him into proposing.

THE WINDUP

The first step toward getting married is saying the word "married" to your boyfriend without prompting him to jump out a window or crap himself (he'll either be dead or too humiliated to ever get naked in front of you again). It's impossible to do this without annoying him, however. Logic would appear to dictate that you pop the M-word cherry while he is at his least annoyable— during the seven minutes of sweaty flopping around he calls sex. Do not do this. There are few things that you as a woman can do to ruin sex for a man. One is to mention his mother, your mother, or any woman who has ever had a baby (especially Reese Witherspoon). The second is to mention marriage. But you're not far off target. You need to be subtle. Wait for your biannual round of oral sex. After he has put an illustrious end to it, say the following words: "I always thought two weeks of this would be the best honeymoon present I could give my husband." Yes, it's a lie—a blatant, not exactly believable lie, but you have caught him at his most vulnerable—and most gullible. And you have planted a seed while he has planted his.

For those unable to stomach the above, you may be surprised to hear that the best way to broach the subject of marriage with a man is the direct way. By "direct," we don't mean shrill. Do not under any circumstances utter the words, "Where is my fucking ring?" or, "Where the fuck is my ring?" or any variation on such.

"Direct" means sitting down with your fella at a low-stress moment (hint: not on a work night and not while the Packers are losing) and talking honestly with him about spending the next few years of your life acting like you'll spend the rest of them together. Here are some good and bad conversation starters:

Good move: Offer to pick up dinner and take him to a place he wants to go to. This doesn't mean you have to head down to O'Flannahannahan's for a basket of atomic wings and a pitcher of Genesee Cream Ale (though that wouldn't hurt). Just think back to dinners he's taken you on where his reaction to the food didn't seem forced or pouty. Remember that Catalan place where you split the giant squid-ink paella and a bottle of Spanish wine? He liked that, because the food looked like dead animals and was served in a frying pan. The key to this is not making it seem like you're taking him to dinner because you have something to talk to him about. Do not say, "I have something to talk to you about." This will put him in panic mode. Let the conversation happen naturally. Let him lead with some subjects; let yourself lead with others. This way, in between the main course and dessert, it won't seem like a trap when you say, "I've been thinking a lot about what you mean to me." Don't use phrases like "our future." The future, as *An Inconvenient Truth* and other science fiction movies have taught us, is scary. Make it about him and how much you love him. The M-word will start being batted around like a birdie at a drunken badminton tournament.

Bad move: Do not walk him by the window at Tiffany and point at diamond rings like a nine-year-old in the Barbie aisle at Toys "R" Us. Nothing is as sickening to a man as seeing the woman he's been boning act like a child. Why? Because it makes him feel like a pederast. Seriously. Men don't want to be your daddy. Your daddy put you through college and taught you how to ride a bike. Your boyfriend and prospective husband wants to do none of those things. He just wants to touch your boobies—over and over again.

Good move: Go fishing with him. All men love to fish. Not all men know how to do it, but tell a guy, "Hey, you want to go spend four hours sitting in the sun and not talking today?" and he'll be out the door and on his way to buy a Zebco starter rod for you before you finish the sentence. The key to fishing with a guy is in choosing your words carefully. Do not take this as an opportunity to have a long conversation. Simply spend the day talking when he wants to talk. By the end of it, he'll be glowing like he just spent the afternoon in a tryst with '80s Heather Locklear and '50s Shirley MacLaine. It is then, on the way home, when you can address the prospect of spending a lot more time together. Like forever. Just say, "I really enjoy spending time with you." Because you didn't spend the day talking him into a coma, he'll say he enjoys spending time with you, too. And he'll mean it.

Bad move: Do not replace the copies of *Maxim* on top of the toilet with a stack of bridal magazines. He needs those *Maxims*. Why? Because he's a ridiculous child. But he's your ridiculous child, and you're not going to get him to entertain the idea of a life with you by getting rid of the stupid things he likes. Deep down, he knows they're stupid. But these are the things that define him as an individual—and also the things he masturbates to when you're angry at him.

Good move: Talk about marriage while visiting his family. Despite the fact that his mother's constant phone calls and his fourteen-year-old sister's meth-addict boyfriend annoy the shit out of him, there is no place where your man is more comfortable than in the home he grew up in. Here he can walk around freely in his underwear and leave half-eaten plates of food anywhere—the couch, the floor, on top of the toilet tank—knowing that someone who is not you will clean up after him without a peep of complaint. It is here, at night after the parents have gone to bed and little sis has climbed out her bedroom window to see Emilio, where you attack: "It's so nice to feel a part of your family." You don't really feel that way, of course—the fact that his mother keeps calling you by his high school girlfriend's name sure isn't helping matters—but he doesn't have to know that.

Bad move: Do not point to your parents as an example of a successful marriage. No matter how healthy their relationship is (really, you call that healthy?), it's the exact opposite of what he wants in a life. Why? Because it's your parents' lives, and they are the enemy. Offering him the chance to spend the next forty years slowly turning into your father isn't exactly going to inspire him to head to Zales.

Victory in sight

The point of these exercises is to make the M-word part of the language you speak to each other. Once you've become accustomed to your new vernacular and you begin to drop sentences like, "My grandmother had a beautiful engagement ring," "We would make awesome little babies," "I've always imagined getting married in the giant megachurch they just built by the interstate off-ramp," and "Sure, I think fall '09 is the perfect time for a wedding," you know that a proposal is soon coming your way.

Your Ring Finger Is Still Bare

Ladies, despite your best efforts, if your hints about wanting to get married aren't picked up on after a year or two, it might be best to just be bold and ask him where he sees this relationship going. If all you want to do is get married and become a breeder, and the man you're currently with doesn't, you (and your rapidly aging ovaries) will thank yourself later for womaning up and finding out where you stand, no matter how pathetic it makes you seem at the time. The word "bummer" doesn't even begin to express our condolences if his response is not what you wanted. On the upside, if you do leave the relationship because of this, there is still a very real possibility that after a few months of abject loneliness, your beau will rethink his stance and do everything imaginable to get you back. Sure, ten years into your marriage he will curse himself for ever being so weak, but what do you care? You have a marriage, house, and babies. All you ever wanted. You win.

. . . .

WE'RE MOVING TOO FAST! TOO FAST!

Ladies, if you want nothing to do with the nonsense we've been spouting—good for you. You probably don't understand the voices that are bellowing out of your lower gut, "I do not want this! I cannot fathom spending every single blessed day together before one of us goes through the horrible stages of death! I now understand why Julia Roberts starred in *The Runaway Bride*." Fellas, if you are with a lady like this and still want to marry her, we'll give you a tip: the best way to quiet that little internal voice of hers is to distract it with something sparkly—an engagement ring. Not to say that women are like raccoons, but, wow, are they ever genetically programmed to like sparkly things.

Which brings us to the proposal section of this book. Men, this is your true moment to actually do something you've been told you will have to do as a man (and really, you've kind of failed at everything else). You will have to propose to your lady. You might think your girlfriend is cool and doesn't have unrealistic, fantasy-based ideas about romance and would rather the proposal thing be laid-back or kind of funny. You're wrong.

See, your girlfriend has probably settled on the fact that you continue to play video games with the glee of a fifteen-year-old. That she will make more money than you. That she will bear the burden of keeping a clean home, a family, and learning how to perform basic home repairs while you (yes, you) sit on the couch watching Sunday/Monday/Friday-night football games. So even though you act like a boy in real life, act like a man when you ask her to marry you. It's the least you can do for the poor thing.

Manning up for the proposal is important, because if she says yes, you will have no say in the planning of the nuptials. You will be relegated to even more childlike status for the ensuing months. When your fiancée finally asks your opinion on whether purple or red carnations are appropriate table settings, your answer will be greeted with an eye roll and a deep sigh, as if you just made a mess in the corner. The proposal is the one aspect in this stage of your life that you will have complete control over. Don't blow it.

Proposing marriage for dipshits

First and foremost, make sure you have a 99 percent chance of her saying yes. You really don't want to be put in the position of having "CARLA WILL YOU MARRY ME?" blasted onto the Jumbo-Tron in the middle of a nationally televised Cubs game only for the whole country to see Carla emphatically shake her head no. Girls don't like huge surprises (and Northsiders, whiny bitches that they are, will blame you for the Cubbies' inevitable late-season collapse). What they do like are heavily orchestrated (and expensive) trips away to romantic locales that incorporate small surprises. If you've prepped them enough, they will have more than a strong inkling as to what will happen when you book a bed-and-breakfast in Vermont during leaf-changing season. Why else are you going? Neither of you like trees or states north of New Jersey. But you both know that you once heard this would be romantic, and you tend to agree with popular opinion. Your honey will be sure to make an appointment to get a manicure right before so her fingernails are painted in a color that matches the magical shade of diamond.

RING-A-DING-DING

When thinking about what kind of ring to get, now is not the time to show off the metallurgical tricks you learned in vocational school. An engagement ring is not a craft project. It is a major purchase that you will be paying off longer than your student loans. By this point, you should know what kind of ring your girlfriend desires. Warning: Do not go into a jewelry shop without this knowledge. If you do, you'll find yourself walking out with a giant dragon pendant emblazoned with semiprecious stones that Yitzhak the jeweler somehow convinced you to purchase. Despite what Yitzhak said, the fact that your girlfriend admires the smooth raps of Ghostface Killah doesn't mean she wants her personal bling to be like his.

Perhaps you are part of a clan that passes down rings from generation to generation. If this is the case, score! You just saved yourself fifteen grand and a shitload of headache. Even if your girlfriend doesn't necessarily find Great-grandma Minnie's ring aesthetically pleasing, she will keep her mouth shut for the rest of eternity because she doesn't want to seem shallow in the face of such almighty tradition.

. . . .

Quiz

Now that you're engaged, should you elope? Take this quiz to find out.

When you call your mother to tell her the good news, she . . .

1. Cries tears of joy. Your mother, unfortunately, has very large tear ducts. All that joy drips down her face and into the cell phone receiver, short-circuiting it. This causes the phone battery to overheat and explode.
2. Cries what she assures you are tears of joy but are actually tears of sadness. She knows you and your bad-influence, heathen mate will never go for the church wedding she's dreamed of since you were born. Making one last effort, she asks when she should call Father Ron to tell him the good news. You answer, "Who?" She cries some more.
3. Cries because that's just what she does. All the time. You can't have all that crying at a wedding.

Your family's most cherished wedding tradition is . . .

1. The horah.
2. Throwing the garter belt.
3. Throwing the thong.

When you sit down to write your wedding vows, the opening line most closely resembles which of the following passages?

1. "There is only one happiness in life, to love and be loved." —George Sand
2. "If I love you, what business is it of yours?" —Johann Wolfgang von Goethe
3. "Love myself better than you." —Kurt Cobain

At your cousin Laura's wedding, your uncle Pat . . .

1. Gives a toast to the bride and groom. His words are brief but poignant. Laura, skinny drama queen that she is, turns on the waterworks and hugs Uncle Pat around the neck. They then dance to "Just the Way You Are" while you hit the open bar for another mojito.
2. Tipped the DJ twenty bucks at the end of the night for honoring his request for a back-to-back playing of "The Chicken Dance."
3. Gives a toast to the bride and groom, but mainly the bride, spending way too much time on how beautiful she looks today, how she's always been the hottest of all his nieces. He slurs, "I mean, just look at her, guys. That nerd she's marrying, he's one lucky son of a bitch tonight—am I right or am I right? Consummate the hell out of that, nerd guy!"

When your intended joined you at your college roommate's country-club wedding, he or she . . .

1. Thought it was charming that they kept it so small. You really get a chance to share a moment with everyone when you keep the guest list limited to four hundred people.
2. Said the fireworks display and horse-drawn carriage were a bit much.
3. Sneaked off to the caddy shack to smoke weed with members of the catering staff.

When your sister was married last year, your parents . . .

1. Sprang for everything, save half the flowers and the rehearsal dinner. The wedding was held at the Hyatt. All the guests stayed free of charge on the fourth floor for the entire week.
2. Pitched in for a small church wedding. "Small" refers to the wedding, the church, and the size of the buffet table.
3. Got wasted and vehemently fought while throwing her wedding gifts at each other's heads. The only gift that didn't break in the melee was the beach ball your father so thoughtfully gave her, which was wrapped in Garfield gift paper.

YOUR RESULTS

Mostly 1s

You and your mate are accustomed to the finer things life has to offer, and your families—well-bred as they are—have always been able to afford them. Go nuts.

Mostly 2s

You can have a proper wedding if you want, but don't expect too much out of it. Just remember: riding through your hometown in the back of a 1942 roadster with rice in your hair isn't all *that* stupendous.

Mostly 3s

For $15 extra, you can get married at city hall when you go to get the marriage license. Throw whatever else you were planning to spend into the honeymoon fund. That's the good part, anyway.

. . . .

HAND TO GOD

In olden times a young man would approach a land-owning gentleman and ask him if he had any nine-year-old daughters lying around. If he did, the land-owning gentleman would say, "Sure thing, but I need a little favor from you . . ." He would then put the young man to work tending his sheep. Seven years later a fatted calf would be slain, the brightest-colored fabrics would be purchased, and a wedding ceremony would ensue. Besides his daughter, the land-owning gentleman would bestow upon his new son-in-law two dozen head of cattle, four goats, and five hectares of prime riverfront property from his personal estate. The couple would then settle into their new digs, where they would bring four children into the world and both die quietly at the age of twenty-six.

Oh, fellas, to live in such times. Nowadays, your girlfriend's dad isn't likely to find you a job—and he doesn't even own any goats. You're left to fend for yourself as you prepare to enter married life. But one thing hasn't changed: you still have to ask the bastard for his daughter's hand.

Yeah, we know, this is the twenty-first century. If you're not getting a fatted-calf dinner out of the deal, you shouldn't have to follow some arcane social ritual. But deep down, every grumpy SOB with a daughter wants the snide boy who's schtupping her to beg a little before he takes her away for good. And life will be a lot easier for you if you make the old man happy. So do yourself a favor. The next time you're stuck on a weekend trip home with the soon-to-be Mrs., ask Pops if he'll grab breakfast with you the morning before you leave. As the two of you sit in the Huddle House quietly digging into your ham and eggs, just blurt out, "So I want to ask Kate to marry me, but I'd like your permission first." Assuming his daughter's name is Kate and he's not a rotten dad, he'll give you an awkward bro-hug and his blessings.

But what if dear old dad is hesitant? If your gal comes from better stock than you, the old man may start peppering you with questions about your finances and whether you think you're ready to give his daughter the kind of life she deserves.

This is the moment all guys dread—and it leaves you with only one option. Stand up from the table slowly, and employ every fiber of your manhood toward making sure your voice doesn't break as you say the following:

"Sir, I wouldn't be speaking with you today if I didn't think I could offer your daughter a good life. I said that I would like your permission to ask her to marry me. I didn't say I needed it."

If that doesn't work, oh well. You're marrying her, not him.

· ·

Just Say Yes

Ladies, it finally happened. Your boyfriend asked you to marry him. The problem is he handed you a Ring Pop and mumbled, "Wanna get married?" then promptly turned his attention back to Photoshopping his college roommate's head onto the bodies of various female porn stars.

Yes, he got the biggest moment of your life entirely fucking wrong. You'd be well within your rights to shove that

Ring Pop juicy jewel of flavor up his urethra and walk away for good. But first you need to ask yourself, "Ten minutes ago, did I want to be married to this man?"

If the answer is yes, you need to just go with it. No, his behavior is not promising. But most men just aren't programmed for wedding proposals. In a perfect world, there would be a service men could hire for sympathetic, Harlequin romance–reading aunts to propose marriage to their girlfriends for them. Those ladies would know how to get it right. But you are stuck dealing with a lunkhead man instead. A sound marriage, should you want it, is more important than a pitch-perfect proposal.

. . . .

. . . .

HE SAYS/SHE SAYS

Should he put three months' salary into an engagement ring?

He Says: Yes! Tradition dictates a man pay three months' salary when he buys an engagement ring for his beloved. I am not exactly a traditional man. I do not own a toolbox. I cannot change the oil in your car. I don't even know why your car needs oil. Isn't it a hybrid, anyway?

I know I didn't pay for our first date and that the only reason I was so eager to move in with you was that I couldn't afford my rent. But that was the old me. The new me is in love with you. The new me wants to grow old with you. The new me is not afraid to sink into thousands of dollars' worth of debt so that you can have a shiny bauble on your finger. What is debt compared to the happiness of the woman I love?

Now, technically, three months of my salary would only get you a $1,900 ring. I know, I keep trying to make the move from substitute teacher to permanent, but so many of these principals are prejudiced against people with face tattoos. Once my lawsuit finally pays off, we'll be living on easy street.

So, for the time being, I don't see a reason not to answer this offer for a $20,000 Discover card and put the entire balance toward your ring. You deserve it, dearest. You, who have stuck with me through thick and through thin, through my lengthy periods of unemployment, through so many holidays with my batshit parents, through that time I rediscovered Ecstasy—you don't deserve just the best I have to offer. You deserve the best that I don't have to offer but through the magic of easy credit can provide.

I want to buy you a ring, darling, a big, fat diamond ring that would choke a horse. Will you marry me?

She Says: No! Sure, it would be nice to know that my eternal love and devotion to you is worth somewhere north of ten grand, but the important thing is that we're going to have a life together, forever and ever. Really! I mean it!

Honey, through these past years, I've come to terms with your faults. I was okay when you dropped out of cooking school when you couldn't figure out how to use an icing gun. And I know that you really didn't mean to get involved in that pyramid scheme and that you were just trying to look out for me when you sold my hybrid on eBay so that you could use the proceeds to buy me "a car that actually starts." I know that you did these things so that we will have a better life. And, sweetie? Hybrids don't start like normal cars. You just have to press a button and it's on. But thanks for looking out for me. You have such a big heart.

All I care about is that you love me. I don't need a giant ring. We're the new breed of bohemians, after all! Diamonds are so establishment! Plus, I'm still paying off Vinnie for your face tattoo, and I don't want to incur much more debt that will make it impossible to move out of your grandmother's house. Let's cut up that little Discover card you found in the mail and make one of your awesome burritos, okay? Tomorrow, we can head to the pawnshop and exchange all of these cooking utensils for a little something that will show the world just how much I appreciate your silly, fucked-up love.

· ·

Finishing Off

Before she wound up a mumbling, pill-infested talking puppet on the world's most successful television show ever, Paula Abdul once asked, "Straight up now tell me are you really going to love me forever? Oh, oh, oh." Emilio Estevez answered, "No." But at least Paula had the balls to ask. Guys and gals, if you want to get married, the most important thing you can do is be "straight up" with your partner. Because if the two of you aren't getting married, you don't want to waste one more day on this relationship. Life is getting shorter every day. Spend the rest of it with someone who doesn't suck.

So you've finished reading this book. It's taken thirty months, and you've plodded through each step at the appropriate pace. You are now a happily married newlywed—and you have no one but us to thank. You're welcome.

Just foolin'. This thing isn't exactly *A People's History of the United States*. Hopefully, you managed to read it in a couple of sittings and reach this epilogue before drunkenly using the pages to light the charcoal at a rooftop barbecue. We appreciate the effort.

Chances are you haven't made it far in the steps described here yet. Maybe you haven't even met a person yet. But when you do—and you will—you'll be better prepared as you go about deciding whether this one's a keeper. If they are, you'll know what to do.

In the meantime, here are a few things to remember no matter what stage of a relationship you're in (we know—like you need any more goddamn advice).

Don't get pissed off. Angry isn't sexy. This is true if you're on the third date or in the third year of a relationship. Like everyone you've ever met, the person you're with will constantly do things to piss you off. Whatever it is, it's not worth getting pissed over.

But wait, you say, whose side are we on anyway? Yours, darling—always yours. We know you're right. We know those sheets cost a lot of money. We know that picture looked great there. We know you loved that dog. But you need to love the person sitting next to you more. Jesus said, "Love thy neighbor"—and who is more neighborly than the person you're banging? No one. And there's a reason you need to love your neighbor: if you don't they're not likely to love you back.

Don't cheat. There are moments in every relationship where the idea of sex with anyone else in the world seems like the best idea since the polio vaccine. But there are a lot of diseases you can pick up from swapping bodily fluids with strangers—and they've made vaccines for very few of them.

We could give you a good finger wagging about the moral implications of cheating. We won't. You can get a finger wagging anywhere. The real reason you shouldn't step out of a relationship, even one that's just a few dates old, is that you do not want to be the person to give someone else VD. The comedic stylings of Sarah Silverman notwithstanding, VD isn't funny. Having it is bad, but giving it to someone who likes you is worse. You want to screw other people that bad? Stay single.

Don't stay too long. As the song says, "breaking up is hard to do." But living a lie is more hard. If at any stage you feel the overwhelming urge to leave, just leave.

"But what if I'm not really unhappy?" you ask. "What if I just have a problem with commitment?" Well then, you have a problem with commitment—and you need to fix it. But you know what doesn't fix a commitment problem? Commitment. Letting a relationship progress to a stage you're not ready for (or staying in a committed relationship you don't want to be in) is like saying, "I'm allergic to bees. I think I'll show my allergy who's boss by harvesting my own honey today." You don't need to throw yourself into the situation that makes your throat close up and your ass swell with hives. You need to go to the doctor and get a shot. Then, later, you can start keeping bees in the backyard. The nice thing about bees is that there are always plenty around for the keeping.

Don't kill yourself. Remember *It's a Wonderful Life*? If Jimmy Stewart hadn't lived, what would have happened to all those townspeople? To be honest, we don't know. We fell asleep in a Christmas turkey coma halfway through the movie. But we're pretty sure it was something shitty.

Killing yourself is never an option. So what if you're lonely and unloved? Maybe someday you won't be. But even if you die alone, at least you'll die of natural causes. And some pretty girl or strapping lad will probably cry at your funeral. So what if it's your sister's kid? Those are real tears.

Even when it sucks, life is awesome. The lonely single still gets to enjoy happy hour, quiet walks on cool evenings, and the occasional late-night happy hour. Someday, we hope you get to experience these things with someone else you really care about.

Until then, keep drinking.

ACKNOWLEDGMENTS

Dorothy would like foremost to thank her wonderful family for their support and love, especially her dad, who taught her the magic of the written word. If anything she writes is half as good and funny as what he has written, she considers herself a lucky gal. She would also like to thank the talented Maris Kreizman for her guidance and tips throughout the whole book-writing process. Thanks also to Ron Varrial, Pat Healy, Josh Cornfield, Kenya Hunt, her New York girls and Philly crew, and especially Brewster Scott for making her totally ineligible to read this book.

Daniel would like to thank his mother, Tanya Holloway; sister, Brooke Elkins; grandmother, Leoni Rocamora; and the rest of his family, all of whom are no doubt shocked and appalled by most of this book (all the curse words are Dorothy's fault, I swear); thanks to the former and current staff of *Metro New York*, especially Kenya Hunt and Michael Ventura; thanks to Milo George and all the good teachers and editors; to Michael Wilkerson, Jeremy Umali, the IPM, and the city of Tallahassee, Florida. Most of all, Daniel would like to thank his wife and best friend, Heidi Albee. (You are the Will Smith to my Tommy Lee Jones. I will roll with you till the wheels fall off.)

From both of us, thanks to Michael Freidson and Maggie Samways—you are our animal spirit guides (or something). Same goes for our agent, Byrd Levell. Why are you so right all the time? Kathy Huck, you are a brave genius for giving this book a home and being an amazing editor. And Matthew Benjamin for being so funny and capable. Thanks to you and everyone at Collins.

Finally, Dorothy and Daniel would like to thank each other for being awesome.